ADVANCE PRAISE FOR

STICKY CASES IN HIGHER EDUCATION LEADERSHIP: ADDRESSING INNOVATION, CHALLENGES, AND CONFLICT

"Everyone knows the adage "If you give someone a fish, you feed them for a day. If you teach them to fish, you feed them for a lifetime." Most leadership books give you the fish in the form of "how to's" for managing various challenges. *Sticky Cases* teaches you to fish by presenting complex, real-world case studies and leaving it to you to determine how best to navigate those challenges. Current and aspiring higher education leaders will benefit from wrestling with these thorny problems, developing skills that will enable them to fish for themselves no matter how choppy the waters of higher education become."

Jacqueline E. King, Ph.D.
Higher Education Leadership and Policy Consultant

"This comprehensive case study book is a must-have resource for higher education professionals, featuring 40 chapters that delve into relevant topics such as Collaboration, Diversity, Equity, and Inclusion, Faculty-Administrator Relationships, and more. The cases are authored by 36 experts, each bringing a unique perspective that enriches the overall content and makes it a valuable resource for classroom use. Each chapter follows a consistent format – areas for reflection, the context, and conflict/challenge; this provides for ease of implementation in the classroom. The discussion questions at the end of each case are thoughtfully crafted to provoke deep reflection and stimulate engaging conversations about the issues presented. This book is not only well-written but also a valuable tool for anyone looking to understand the complexities of today's educational environment."

Dr. Peter J. Mcaliney, Director,
Professional and Executive Education at Rutgers, and Director,
Ragone Center for Excellence in Accounting, Rutgers University

"This wonderful book is a collection of lively and relevant cases suitable for a variety of leadership development programs. The dilemmas will be familiar to anyone in organizations where governance is a combination of applying legal rules, institutional policies, and humanitarian considerations. Thoughtful questions provide a basis for collaborative problem solving and encourage the reader to seek further knowledge. The authors have filled a gap in leadership preparation curriculum with a timely and useful publication."

Rene Parmar, Ph.D.
Dean, School of Education
SUNY New Paltz

"What a great book! I thoroughly enjoyed reading "*Sticky Cases in Higher Education*." The authentic cases shed light on some of the truly contentious issues facing higher education institutions, such as the tension between historical recognition, first nation injustices, and contemporary values. It examines the rhetoric and the actual practice of equity, the realities of accessibility in virtual learning environments, and navigating hierarchical structures to ensure succession planning within university leadership. The cases and accompanying questions are sure to inspire thoughtful reflection and encourage key stakeholders to come together to find proactive solutions to some of the most pressing challenges we face in Higher Education."

Professor Angela Carbone
Associate Deputy Vice Chancellor Learning Teaching and Quality
STEM College, RMIT University, Australia

"In the last fifteen years, the United States has gone through a series of shocks: economic downturn, political turmoil, a racial reckoning, COVID, war in the Middle East. Higher education has not been immune to such unrest. In fact, far from it. And in the North and Midwest, where demographic decline has only sharpened our challenges, higher education leaders must be constantly watchful, thoughtful, and attentive.

We need a guide in such turbulent times, one that helps us think through problems rather than offering ready-made, cookie cutter answers that do not meet the real needs of our institutions. *Sticky Cases* offers just that. This book provides readers with real world cases that require teams of diverse leaders to develop thoughtful responses that meet the demands of the day. For leaders looking for a book that offers an approach to solving real world challenges of today, *Sticky Cases* is mandatory reading."

James Wolfinger, Dean
The School of Education, St. John's University

STICKY CASES IN HIGHER EDUCATION LEADERSHIP

CRITICAL LEADERSHIP PEDAGOGY AND PRAXIS

EDITED BY TRICIA M. KRESS AND WARREN E. WHITAKER

This book series is designed to bridge the divide between critical pedagogy and critical leadership studies by exploring, articulating, and ultimately expanding the praxis of critical pedagogy as leadership. In the narrative tradition of Freire's post-*Pedagogy of the Oppressed* volumes, books in this series capture the in-between of leadership and critical pedagogy through the experiences and stories of contemporary and historical educational leaders. Texts in this series blend of narrative/biographic, empirical, theoretical/conceptual visions of critical pedagogical leadership for education, including biographies/autobiographies of critical educational leaders and administrators; historical and futuristic visions of critical pedagogical leadership and administration in education; and narratives of grassroots leadership of communities, teachers and students. Consistent with critical pedagogy as a philosophy, texts in this series will traverse the boundaries of the theoretical and practical and encourage the conscientizing process of leaders by sharing the stories of contexts, places, and dynamics that are central to living critical leadership praxis.

Forthcoming Titles:

Sticky Cases in Higher Education Leadership: Addressing Innovation, Challenges, and Conflict
Edited by Laurie Bobley, Alan Sebel, and Sabra Brock (2024)

Critical Leadership Praxis for the Future of Democracy
Edited by Warren E. Whitaker, Kathryn Strom, and Tricia Kress (2025)

If you're interested in submitting a proposal for possible inclusion in the series, please contact the series editors, Tricia M. Kress (tkress@molloy.edu) or Warren Whitaker (wwhitaker@molloy.edu).

STICKY CASES IN HIGHER EDUCATION LEADERSHIP

Addressing Innovation, Challenges, and Conflict

EDITED BY LAURIE BOBLEY,
ALAN SEBEL, AND SABRA BROCK

Myers Education Press
Gorham, Maine

Myers Education Press

Published by Myers Education Press, LLC
P.O. Box 424
Gorham, ME 04038

Myers Education Press is an academic publisher specializing in books, e-books, and digital content in the field of education. All of our books are subjected to a rigorous peer review process and produced in compliance with the standards of the Council on Library and Information Resources.

Library of Congress Cataloging-in-Publication Data available from Library of Congress.

13-digit ISBN 978-1-9755-0650-6 (paperback)
13-digit ISBN 978-1-9755-0651-3 (library networkable e-edition)
13-digit ISBN 978-1-9755-0652-0 (consumer e-edition)

Printed in the United States of America.

All first editions printed on acid-free paper that meets the American National Standards Institute Z39-48 standard.

Books published by Myers Education Press may be purchased at special quantity discount rates for groups, workshops, training organizations, and classroom usage. Please call our customer service department at 1-800-232-0223 for details.

Cover design by Teresa Lagrange.

Visit us on the web at **www.myersedpress.com** to browse our complete list of titles.

Contents

Acknowledgments

As the creators and facilitators of the Touro College Academy of Leadership and Management (TCALM), we saw the need for a book of cases that would fill a gap in instructional resources for universities offering and implementing leadership development programs. We want to acknowledge Patricia Salkin, Senior Vice President of Academic Affairs and Provost of the Graduate and Professional Division of Touro University. It was her gracious encouragement and unlimited support that guided us when we proposed and then put into action TCALM. We also want to express our sincere appreciation to the leaders who contributed to this volume. The thought they put into developing meaningful, insightful cases is truly commendable. Our hope is that this book will serve as a valuable resource for current and aspiring higher education leaders, empowering them to navigate the complexities of their roles and drive positive change within their institutions and communities.

Foreword

Nicholas W. Allard[1]

STICKY CASES IN HIGHER EDUCATION *Leadership: Addressing Innovation, Challenges, and Conflict* is an essential addition to the toolbox of anyone who cares about academic leadership and the future of higher education. This fresh new book is well designed to promote robust leadership education and training at a time when the only constants in our lives are accelerating change and daunting, often unexpected, crises. The book, among many potential practical uses, is a veritable Swiss army knife for assembling, customizing, and running "do it yourself" leadership training for academic leadership at every level. Even so, its potential applications go far beyond learning how to lead and could be useful in all sorts of organizations.

In this volume, which could well evolve into a regular series, you will find 40 illustrative, fictionalized but reality-based case studies written by three dozen experienced academic administrators, managers, and faculty from a variety of fields and institutions in the United States and abroad. These short, original, engaging, provocative cases are designed to prompt thinking, conversation, learning, and preparation for a wide spectrum of contemporary issues that arise in the academy. Practice, practice, practice is the punchline to the well-known, well-worn joke question: "How do you get to Carnegie Hall?" When educators ask how to be ready when you can expect the unexpected, an excellent answer is to use *Sticky Cases* to practice, practice, practice.

The editors' curated collection of ready-to-use scenarios also can be readily tailored for the bespoke needs of any university, college, community college, department, institute, or other non-profit organization for that matter. In this regard, the editors and authors of *Sticky Cases* have taken a generous approach writing case studies that can be changed and adapted as desired depending on relevant circumstances.

In addition, being able to rehearse how to analyze and manage responses to knotty problems is in and of itself a valuable exercise. Problem solving drills sharpen skills and confidence that can be beneficial no matter how closely the mock conundrums and team building exercises, as written, or as may be customized by readers, match the circumstances of real challenges that may arise for any specific organization.

Sticky Cases offers no answers or advice. Instead, each short crisp chapter sets the table for working with colleagues cooperatively by reflecting upon and answering questions about provocative fact patterns containing interesting, but necessarily incomplete information. There are prompts designed to help readers and workshop participants identify and discuss conflicts, weigh options, assess risks and benefits, and consider how to develop and execute a plan. In my view there is no other book about academic leadership quite like it and nothing of this kind since the disruption of the global pandemic.

The importance of this unique collection of leadership scripts should be self-evident. For the remainder of this decade, and as far ahead as our vision can perceive in the 21st century, every sector, including higher education, will be buffeted by the same chaos, uncertainty, and political and cultural polarization, as well as disturbing dangerous threats to people everywhere. For the foreseeable future, disruptive change for good and bad, divisiveness, unrest, tumult, violence, and human-made and natural emergencies are givens.

Accordingly, the most successful educators will need to focus on three priorities:

Value: We can no longer take for granted that higher education is considered a springboard to the American Dream. For the first time in living memory, despite compelling evidence to the contrary, it is increasingly common for people to doubt the worth of a post-secondary degree. Successful educators must be able to articulate the value proposition of their institution in terms of lifelong earnings, professional accomplishments, and accolades. It also is imperative that they champion the intangibles such as the value of knowledge, self-worth, satisfaction, and the gratification of meaningful service to others. As Princeton's former president, renowned scientist Dr. Shirley Tilghman has said, the arts and humanities are priceless. In combination with STEMM subjects, they are vaccines for protecting humanity from obsolescence, irrelevance, inequality, authoritarianism, economic distress, exploitation, unethical behavior, injustice, and other dangers.

Adaptation: Successful educators will prepare students and constantly engage in fact-based adjustments of teaching and scholarship. They must address and prepare graduates both for the world as we know it, but also as important, promote lifelong learning skills that equip people with the knowledge and critical thinking needed to adapt to the continuous disruptive change, including, specifically, to qualify graduates for careers and to tackle challenges that do not yet exist.

Purpose: Understandably, academic faculty, staff, and students are troubled and distracted by the seemingly hopelessness of the many upsetting issues of our times. They may feel like our world is falling apart as if there will be no tomorrow. They worry about their own safety and the suffering of others. It is important for leaders to remind academic communities, without downplaying the seriousness of contemporary problems, that the world has always been full of troubles, and it always will be. They also should help people to be mindful about the purpose and the opportunity they will have to use what they are learning to make the world better. Afterall, academic institutions have been throughout history the field hospitals for what ails society. In other words, it is important to spotlight that what the people of each academic community are doing is important and matters.

In pursuit of these objectives, *Sticky Cases* is a timely book that can be a resource for everyone involved in handling the demands of an academic job. For example, at our new College of Law launched only two years ago, we will be able to use the book to organize breakout workshops when our leadership team and faculty gather offsite for what usually is called a "retreat" but instead we refer to as our "charge," underscoring our intentional forward-looking focus. It is not hard to think about other uses of the materials including possibly in hiring and onboarding faculty and staff, assimilating adjuncts, training sessions for human resources and legal compliance, and, of course, as reading materials in leadership courses.

If I may be permitted a personal note, I can report that although I am enormously impressed by *Sticky Cases*, and grateful to now have it on my shelf, I am not surprised. For several years I have had the privilege of participating in the extraordinary work of those who have been involved with leadership education and the annual exercise that soon will be renamed the Leadership Academy at Touro University. This includes my dear friend and path clearing author in her own right, Dr. Patricia E. Salkin, the senior vice president for Academic Affairs and Provost of the Graduate and Professional Division of Touro University. I am indebted to Patty, a former fellow law dean and New Yorker, for first drawing me into Touro's exceptional leadership training program. I had high expectations for this book because of my own experience over several years working with the three editors, Drs. Bobley, Sebel, and Brock whose names are on the cover, and with many of the authors of the 40 chapters between covers. *Sticky Cases* exceeds all expectations and then some.

Note

1. **Nicholas W. Allard** is an educator and lawyer with national and international prominence in higher education, public policy, U.S. and international government relations, technology, and innovation. He is the Founding Randall C. Berg, Jr. Dean of the Jacksonville University College of Law which welcomed its first students in 2022 and received its initial American Bar Association accreditation in early 2024. "Nick" served as Joseph Crea Dean (2012-18) and concurrently as President (2013-18) at Brooklyn Law School (BLS). At Jacksonville University he is a tenured professor of law and on the faculty of the University's Public Policy Institute. Nick's work in government service, higher education, and numerous volunteer leadership roles has straddled partnerships in some of the world's most highly regarded law firms. He is a graduate of Princeton's School of Policy and International Affairs, Oxford as a Rhodes Scholar earning an M.A. in Politics, Philosophy and Economics, and Yale Law School.

Introduction

THIS IS A BOOK BY leaders for leaders. It was conceived by the editors as an outgrowth of a faculty leadership development program they initiated and facilitated at their institution. National accreditors such as the Middle States Commission on Higher Education expect universities to focus on succession planning and institutional renewal, including the internal development of leaders. In the world of education this is often referred to as "grow your own," where organizations seek to identify current employees who show the potential and the desire to rise in rank.

During their work with aspiring and practicing leaders, the editors quickly found that there is a shortage of case study books specific to leadership development in higher education. Case study analysis allows for the practice and refinement of the skills necessary for assuming higher level positions. Further, "one of the best ways to apply and understand theoretical concepts is through experiential learning rooted in the use of case studies" (Northouse & Lee, 2016, p. 3).

Case study analysis reveals the complexities that leaders in any position encounter. It demonstrates how each action may result in planned or unexpected outcomes, and it can highlight new challenges or opportunities. When using case studies, "the professor can encourage moral reasoning, critical thinking and problem solving" (Kowalski, 2012, p. xiv). This volume is a collection of case studies written by faculty and academic leaders, some of whom have completed a faculty leadership and management development program and currently serve in leadership roles. Additional cases were contributed by faculty and academic leaders from other higher education institutions within the United States and internationally. Some of the cases are set in organizations outside higher education. They are included because leadership spans time, space, and place. As an extension, the challenges faced and choices made by leaders can provide valuable lessons regardless of the business or industry of the organization.

The purpose of this book is to provide additional material to universities offering programs in higher education leadership development. Other audiences are colleges or universities that, as part of their succession planning, currently have or are preparing to initiate leadership development programs. This collection is designed to be used as a teaching tool in multiple settings, including doctoral and master's degree programs that focus on higher education leadership and management.

The cases will enrich the experience of the program participants and can be aligned with program outcomes and professional standards. The cases are open-ended to encourage thoughtful independent or collaborative thinking about the situations that are described. Readers have the opportunity to analyze authentic situations and propose solutions or alternative approaches to address the issues presented.

Each case offers areas for reflection, background information to provide context, a leadership challenge or conflict, and questions for consideration. The areas for reflection and the questions are provided to guide readers as the cases are analyzed. The cases can be used whether the class is conducted in-person, asynchronously online, or in a blended format. Instructors may find it useful to include more than one case in a particular class or assign different cases to teams for a more nuanced and complex discussion. The latter option simulates those situations in which academic leaders are faced with a multitude of issues at the same time.

In the case title, we have tried to identify the underlying issues so that users can more easily locate cases relevant to the learning points of their course. The cases are arranged by areas for reflection and grouped as follows: Collaboration; Diversity, Equity and Inclusion; Faculty-Administrator Relationships; Implementing and Adapting to Change; Introducing New Technologies; Overcoming Performance Issues; and Professional Growth. The cases in these groupings touch on topics such as administrative discretion, administrative disfunction, peer supervision, faculty discretion, policy vs. practice, ethical considerations, procedural clarity, institutional culture, academic integrity, fiscal considerations, technology integration, and pedagogy, among others.

While the cases are reflective of situations that a leader in any institution of higher education might experience, they are not attributable to any specific institution or individual. Proper names of colleges, universities, organizations, and individuals are fictitious, with the exception of Chapter 6 which identifies an actual institution. Additionally, three of the cases were developed with the assistance of generative AI. The editor of each of those cases input the factors to be addressed and the format of the cases in the book, and then AI generated a draft, which was further edited and refined by the editor.

References

Kowalski, T. J. (2012). *Case studies in educational administration*. Allyn Bacon.

Northouse, P. G., & Lee, M. (2016). *Leadership case studies in education*. Sage.

PART I

COLLABORATION

ONE

Ethical Leadership Conflict

Alan Sebel

AREAS FOR REFLECTION

- Policy vs. practice
- Administrative discretion
- Leadership style
- Faculty/administrator relationships

The Context

The Executive Leadership program is housed in a Graduate School of Business at a premier university in Boston. The program prepares students for executive positions in major corporations throughout the nation and internationally. Applicants to the program must be supported by their current employers, and often the employer pays all or part of the student's tuition. At the time of this incident the program had an enrollment of approximately 150 students, all of whom are already in significant leadership positions at their current place of employment. There are three full-time faculty members including the chairperson and two adjunct faculty members. The chair reports to the dean of the Graduate School of Business. The University has a clearly defined Academic Integrity Policy that includes possible penalties if a student violates the policy. The penalty can range from failure of a course to expulsion from the University. In this case the concept of administrative discretion becomes a factor in the actions of the chairperson. Administrative discretion is defined as "the exercise of professional expertise and judgement, as opposed to strict adherence to regulations or statutes, in making a decision or performing official acts or duties" (Administrative, 2008).

Dr. Able teaches the first course in the leadership program's sequence of courses. He has been at the University for more than 20 years. He always receives strong evaluations from his students, serves as a peer mentor to other faculty in their use of online education, and conducts peer reviews. He worked with the chairperson for his entire time at the University, and before that, they both served in the same international corporation where the chairperson had been the direct supervisor of Dr. Able. After retirement the chairperson was asked to join the University, and a short time later, she asked Dr. Able to join her. They have an excellent collaborative working relationship and hold each other in high esteem.

It is now the fourth week of the spring semester. Dr. Able is reading and grading the week's assignment submissions. He is reading the work of Alyssa. Throughout the first three weeks of the term, Alyssa's work showed increasing improvement. On the first three assignments she has earned a B+, A-, and an A. As he reads the current submission, he is troubled as it seems remarkably similar to another student's work he has previously read. He reads it again and he is sure that he has read this before. All written coursework is submitted through the University's Learning Management System (LMS) and goes through the LMS plagiarism check system. At the start of each semester, students are required to affirm that they will comply with the University's Academic Integrity Policy. Dr. Able will not read and grade student work at the start of the semester until the student has made this affirmation. This is clearly noted in class and in the course syllabus. Upon growing suspicious about the originality of Alyssa's latest work, Dr. Able accesses the plagiarism report and sees that it identifies that 85% of the paper is the same as work submitted by another student in the program two semesters ago. The professor now goes back to the three assignments previously submitted by Alyssa. These appear to be Alyssa's original work.

So that students and the professor can learn about each other's personal and professional background, each class member posts a brief biography and states what they hope to achieve as a result of being in the program. Dr. Able decides to reread Alyssa's "Getting to Know You" discussion board post from the first week of the semester. The professor sees that the student works at Memory Corporation, and she states that she was encouraged to enter the program by her colleague, Jacki. The professor suspects that Jacki, who is still in the program, may be the author of the original paper.

Dr. Able pulls up the work that was previously submitted by Jacki two semesters ago and compares the two works. He determines that Alyssa has in fact plagiarized, or Jacki has shared the paper with her, and Alyssa has only minimally changed the content of the paper to make it appear original. He asked to meet with the chairperson. He prints out copies of the two papers in question and the previous three assignments. Although they were not identified as being significantly copied from another's work, there are segments of each paper that are clearly paraphrased from Jacki's work. He is concerned that he had not recognized this earlier.

At the meeting, the chair reviews the papers and sees the similarities. The chair asks Dr. Able if he routinely uses the same assignment each semester. He responds that he rotates the case study assignments each term. However, given the time between when the two students were in the course, the assignment would have been the same. Clearly, if he had selected entirely different case studies each semester, the current situation would not have occurred.

Dr. Able urges the chair to expel both students, believing that Alyssa could not have been able to copy the work of her colleague without Jacki knowingly providing her work to Alyssa. He believes they are in violation of the University's Academic Integrity Policy and should be expelled from it in accordance with the policy. The chair urges him to have a meeting with Alyssa, present the evidence, give her an F for the assignment, and let her complete the course. The chair does not see the need to discipline the originator of the work, noting that she is completing her coursework and preparing for graduation. The chair states that doing so, if it became public knowledge, might negatively impact Jacki's career. Dr. Able refuses to do what the chair suggests and insists that disciplinary action be taken by the chair. This is the first time in a relationship of more than 30 years that these professionals have had a significant disagreement.

The Conflict/Challenge

Dr. Able is determined that both students should be penalized by being expelled from the program. In an attempt to bring resolution to the situation, the chair suggests that Alyssa be given an F for the assignment in question and be required to complete alternative assignments for the first three pieces of writing that had similar content to that of Jacki's work. These would be graded by Dr. Able with penalties. Alyssa will be told that any further use of the work of others without appropriate affirmation will result in expulsion. The other professors who have Alyssa as a student in their courses are advised to closely review her work to assess if any of her work is not original. The chair determines that other than having a conversation with Jacki, she will not act against her.

At a faculty meeting, Dr. Able challenges these decisions. He states that this sends the wrong message to all students about the policy of the University. He also states that the penalty suggested only really creates new work for him and his peers and lets both students off without any real penalty for their unprofessional and unethical behavior. The other professors agree that this is setting a poor example for other Graduate School of Business students. Finally, Dr. Able tells the chair that he is disappointed and that he is going to bring this to the attention of the dean of the Graduate School of Business.

Questions for Discussion

1. Did the chairperson make the correct decision about how the apparent sharing of work between Alyssa and Jacki was addressed?
2. Considering that Dr. Able informed the chairperson that he was escalating this to the dean, what next steps should the chairperson take?
3. Is the professor at all culpable for this happening? Why or why not?
4. What might the impact be on the program's historic cohesiveness?
5. If the chairperson allows the students to remain in the program without consequences for their actions, how might this impact the integrity of the program going forward?
6. Is there a place for administrative discretion when implementing set organization policy? Why or why not?

Reference

Administrative Discretion. (2008.) *West's encyclopedia of American law*, (2nd ed.). encyclopedia.com

TWO

Advancing Your Agenda

Marian Stotz-Loike

AREAS FOR REFLECTION

- Implementing change
- Developing peer relationships
- Instituting faculty professional development

The Context

THE PRIMARY FOCUS OF THE Department of Online Education has been on training faculty to teach asynchronous online courses. This involved creating a rubric as well as several courses to enable faculty to master the skills necessary to be pedagogically successful in teaching these remotely.

Since the COVID-19 pandemic, the University has offered more classes that were held using video conference technologies, and faculty have needed more remote education skills, even if they were teaching primarily in a classroom.

During the pandemic, the Instructional Design team that operates as part of the Department of Online Education developed several self-paced, asynchronous courses known as the *Faculty Development Tools in Zoom and Canvas.* These courses have four levels—Bronze, Silver, Gold, and Platinum—preparing faculty to use Zoom and Canvas through training material offered in text or video, with the levels increasing in complexity. Faculty are given a mastery quiz when they complete each level and receive badges for completion.

When all classes moved online or to video conference during the pandemic, it became obvious that every faculty member had to complete these courses. Between 80% and 90% of graduate faculty have completed the *Faculty Development Tools* courses at the Bronze and Silver levels. Because any faculty member interested in teaching a fully online module or a fully online course must complete the Gold level of the *Faculty Development Tools*, more than 70% have completed that level. Platinum was released only recently, so faculty are still engaged in building mastery.

As an outgrowth of health and safety steps taken during the pandemic, video conference has become a more viable option for continuing instruction for many reasons. For example, both faculty and students are more likely to stay home when they are ill but can now continue to attend classes; faculty traveling to conferences can still attend important meetings; and cancelling classes for snow days is no longer necessary. Video conferencing technologies such as Zoom offer an opportunity to maintain class continuity.

New faculty members may not have the skills required for classroom or remote education. During the pandemic, remote education skills were of primary importance because students could not attend class in person. Because there is no longer a pandemic crisis, many other issues vie with the need for faculty to build remote education skills.

Before the pandemic, the vice president for Online Education built strong relationships with deans and program chairs by serving on search committees for deans and other senior leaders at several of the graduate schools. Additionally, the vice president often attended programs at the graduate and professional schools to show her support.

During the pandemic, those relationships grew stronger and deeper. The executive vice president and provost held daily Academic Continuity meetings that enabled the senior leadership of the University to brainstorm and solve problems together. Additionally, the vice president presented regularly to the group about programs and material that her team was developing in support of educational success across schools. In fact, the vice president created a unique program called i-LIVE (Leadership in Virtual Education) with support of two academic leaders to prepare the senior leadership of the University to become more successful in leading in a remote education environment. Experts from foundations, industry, academia, and the private sector joined participants to discuss critical educational issues. Through these efforts, the Department of Online Education built goodwill and trust across the University, enabling the department to be viewed as a critical educational resource.

The Conflict/Challenge

After students returned to the classroom, the vice president approached the Provost to recommend that all new faculty be required to complete at least the Bronze, Silver, and Gold Levels of the *Faculty Development Tools*. The provost felt that that was a decision that needed to be approved at a meeting of the deans of the Graduate and Professional schools.

While the provost's opinion made sense, the vice president recognized that she could move the needle toward "yes" by leveraging her relationships with the deans. She met through video conference with every dean to solicit feedback regarding requiring all faculty members, including new hires, to complete the *Faculty Development Tools* course within the next semester.

Because there are many new faculty hired each semester, at the deans' quarterly meeting, they agreed to require all new faculty to take the *Faculty Development Tools* course within one semester of being hired.

Despite the support from leadership, one semester after the decision to require this training, metrics showed that only 35% of new faculty had completed up to the Gold level.

Questions for Discussion

1. In an institution of higher education, who is responsible for lobbying to introduce faculty training for technology innovations, such as AI (Artificial Intelligence), that can serve to upgrade teaching and student learning?
2. How can a leader motivate faculty to accept innovations that might improve their teaching, despite their resistance?
3. In reviewing the small percentage of new faculty completing the *Faculty Development Tools* course, what should the VP of Online Education do next?
4. How do you motivate new faculty, including adjuncts, to complete tasks that are beyond the teaching responsibilities they expect?
5. What might you do to build relationships across departments/schools/leaders, and how can you leverage those relationships to advance change?

THREE

Bridging the Communication Gap[1]

Sabra Brock

> **AREAS FOR REFLECTION**
>
> - Honoring donor intent
> - Communication among idiosyncratic systems
> - Contingencies for unique student needs

The Context

IN AN AGE WHERE TECHNOLOGY is integral to the functioning of educational institutions, the incident at Towne College raises fundamental questions about the seamless operation of various systems and the stewardship of donations. This case revolves around the generous donation of $1000, intended for a graduate business student to study at Towne College's sister school in Rome, Italy. Both campuses shared identical curricula, and an agreement existed to credit tuition payments made at one campus to the other. Despite these seemingly straightforward arrangements, this incident underscores the challenges that arise when technological systems within an institution fail to communicate effectively.

The situation at Towne College highlights the need to reconcile the intersection of technology platforms and donations. As educational institutions continue to rely on various technological systems for seamless operations, these systems must be capable of communicating with each other. Moreover, institutions should establish clear guidelines for handling donations and consider the creation of emergency funds to support students in need when technological incompatibilities hinder the intended use of donated funds. This case serves as a reminder of the importance of putting humanity back into technology, ensuring that the welfare and educational pursuits of students remain at the forefront of institutional decision-making.

The Conflict/Challenge

The conflict at the heart of this case arose when the student recipient of the donor's scholarship attempted to access the donated funds to cover her airfare expenses for her semester abroad in Rome. She waited until the last possible day to book the flight. Payment was denied, as the contribution had been allocated to the College's Development Department's budget. The function of the Development Department is to solicit, attract, and distribute funds to recipients of grants and scholarships. The head of the Development Department expressed empathy towards the students' situation but explained that the budget had been closed for the year, and the donation was housed within a general budget, complicating the release of funds. This left the student in a precarious situation, as she had already secured housing in Rome and counted on the $1000 for her travel expenses.

Questions for Discussion

1. Is the response of the head of the Development Department ethical as it relates to the donor and the student? What if any ethical principles are being violated in this case?
2. If problems result when the various technology platforms of an institution negatively impact an individual or a department, what recourse exists?
3. Who has responsibility for ensuring that donations to an institution are used for their intended purpose?
4. What is the responsibility of an institution to set up emergency funds that can be used when a system's incompatibility prevents their intended use?

Note:

1. This case was generated by ChatGPT with prompts provided by the author/editor. AI (Artificial Intelligence) provided the foundation of the case, and the author/editor refined the content.

FOUR

Same Page: Building Common Understandings in Program Design

Marcella Bullmaster-Day

AREAS FOR REFLECTION

- Program design leadership
- Interactive discussion strategies
- Building a culture of collaboration

The Context

AT THE TIME OF THIS incident, the Mountain Top University Master of Science degree program in Early Childhood Education comprised 12 graduate courses, enrolled approximately 500 Master of Science degree candidates in each academic term (fall, spring, summer), and offered each course each term in multiple sections and formats. Courses could be taken in-person or video conference, across five campus locations, asynchronously or online. Approximately 25 different instructors (full-time faculty, adjuncts, and field supervisors) taught these courses each term.

The associate dean of Academic Affairs recognized a need to ensure greater coherence and comparable quality of degree candidates' learning experiences through the Early Childhood program. She conducted a one-hour interactive session with all Early Childhood instructors and site administrators/advisors for the purpose of beginning to collaboratively build mutual understandings of: final program performance outcomes; the rationale for the sequence of courses; and how each course's assignments/learning experiences built upon previous courses and prepared candidates for future courses to ensure that candidates were developing the knowledge, skills, and dispositions required to achieve the final program outcomes.

The session was held in a classroom with 16 instructors attending in person and another eight instructors participating via Zoom from other campuses. In the absence of an electronic smartboard device and using only paper, the front wall served as the visual center of the meeting.

Across the wall from left to right were these items: multiple pieces of tape, followed by a row of 12 sheets of 8.5"x11" paper, followed by pictures of young children above a large poster paper that read, "What do young children need?" This was followed by pictures of teachers above another poster paper reading, "What do teachers need?" Under the row of 12 blank sheets was a random grouping of adhesive-backed notes, each with the name of one of the program's courses. For this meeting, the associate dean followed her planned agenda, laid out in segments with allotted minutes for each segment. A colleague assisted by keeping time for each segment so that the group would stay on track with the activities.

Arriving at the door, instructors picked up the agenda for the meeting and a cut-out paper figure (printed from the Internet, photos of diverse young adults). The associate dean asked them to let this "paper doll" represent a degree candidate they had taught, and to write the first name and a few descriptors of that individual on the back of the paper figure. The associate dean began the conversation at the poster paper under pictures of children with the question, "What do young children need for healthy development academically, emotionally, socially, and physically?" Answers flowed enthusiastically in "popcorn" response style, and the associate dean jotted them as quickly as she could, filling the large paper. "Young children need self-confidence . . . self-esteem . . . trust . . . caring . . . empathy . . . differentiated instruction . . . social skills . . . to feel safe . . . healthy food . . . self-regulation . . . attention . . . focus . . . engaging tasks that are meaningful to them . . . to be read to . . . enrichment activities . . . play . . . parent involvement . . . curiosity . . . educational toys . . . to go outside to be in touch with nature . . . art and music . . . medical preventative measures . . . sleep . . . health and hygiene. . . ."

Next, moving to the poster under pictures of teachers, the associate dean asked, "So if the children need these things, what do the teachers need in order to serve these children?" Again, participants answered thoughtfully and vigorously as the associate dean jotted the responses: "They need knowledge of the child's environment . . . resource materials and an understanding of how to use them in the classroom . . . administration's support . . . books . . . technology . . . toys . . . to understand what to expect from kids, child development knowledge . . . cultural understanding . . . collaboration with parents . . . diplomacy . . . kindness . . . positive communication skills . . . they need to like children . . . understand spectrums of abilities . . . to be emotionally healthy . . . ability to differentiate instruction . . . knowledge of multiple teaching strategies . . . to be open-minded . . . patient . . . high-energy . . . able to assess students' learning and use assessment to inform instruction . . . theory, practice, research . . . curriculum and how to support it . . . state requirements . . . professional standards . . . existing models or/approaches to early childhood education . . . early intervention measures. . . ."

Now that the introductory activity was completed, the associate dean asked participants to introduce both themselves and their "paper doll" representing one of their candidates. As they did this, they handed the associate dean the paper figures, and she taped these to the wall ahead of the sequence of courses so that the visual represented these degree candidates as ready to begin moving through the 12 courses laid out in front of them.

Examples of instructors' introductions of their candidates included, "This is Eric. He is from the Midwest and his previous career was in technology as a web designer, and he spent one year in the Peace Corps." "My candidate is Tonya. English is not her first language, she teaches in a private school; she believes that the Master of Science degree program in Early Childhood will be the easiest program, and that she will finish very quickly and find a job." "My candidate is Nick; he majored in business and when his music business was not what he wanted, he decided to become a teacher. He plans to apply to the School Leadership program once he is certified and experienced." "Sarah is a 24-year-old single mom who dropped out of college for a time with substance abuse issues, then finished and wants to be an early childhood teacher to ensure children a strong start." "Mary has been an assistant teacher for 15 years and she thinks she knows everything, yet I see where she can use additional growth in many areas." "Jaqueline is an ideal candidate—attentive, creative, and hard-working."

Pointing to the array of these paper figures on the wall, the associate dean asked, "What do you notice about these individuals?" Immediately, the response was, "None of them are the same." They were diverse in every way: age, gender, race, language, experience, and what brought them to the Master of Science degree program. The associate dean pointed to the group of figures and then walked to the other end of the program course sequence to point to the poster on "What Teachers Need" and said, "So we know that this diverse group of aspiring Early Childhood teachers need to come out of our Master of Science degree program with the knowledge, skills, and dispositions that you have identified in order to support children in getting what they need."

Her next question was, "So where should they start? Which courses first, and why? And then which courses should follow?" From there the very lively group discussion unfurled based on participants' arguments for the order in which courses should be taken and why certain courses needed to precede or follow others. As they came to agreement, she placed the course-name sticky notes on the 12 sheets of paper so that, at the end, the group had established an agreed-upon sequence of courses from which to produce a revised Program Roadmap for degree candidates.

This 60-minute interactive session was just one whole-group conversation intended to start ongoing discussions about ensuring that degree candidates would build comparable knowledge, skills, and dispositions no matter at what location or in what format they completed their courses. This would require instructors and advisers to understand program outcomes and how each course fits into the sequence of candidates' learning experiences as they move through the degree program.

The Conflict/Challenge

The challenge was how to follow up to establish and maintain a continuing system of regular communication among 25 Early Childhood program instructors and administrators working at separate university sites across the five distant locations, as well as asynchronously online. Best practices for collaboratively building mutual understanding across teams in learning organizations include regular opportunities to strengthen shared vision; to improve methods, materials, and results; and to allow all stakeholders' voices to be heard (Senge, 2000; Sutton & Shouse, 2016; Zasa & Buganza, 2022). Regular monthly video conference meetings with clear agendas, visuals, discussions, and minutes were established. However, time limitations and the large number of instructors and advisors across locations made coherence challenging, as not all instructors, especially adjuncts, could attend every meeting; each campus location had formed its own internal culture; instructors had determined their own preferred course content, which could differ widely across sections of the same course; and large meetings did not always allow for all participants to contribute.

Questions for Discussion

1. What are the basic elements of program design?
2. How did the interactive flow of this one-hour session keep participants engaged? Would you use other strategies?
3. What elements are necessary for building an ongoing professional learning community over time when colleagues do not work together at the same site location?
4. How would you involve adjunct faculty in the professional learning community?
5. Given the fact that a course taught by several faculty members did not have consistent content, how could the program ensure consistency of degree candidate learning outcomes?

References

Senge, P. (2000) *Schools that learn. A fifth discipline field book for educators, parents, and everyone who cares about education.* Doubleday.

Sutton, P. S., & Shouse, A. W. (2016). Building a culture of collaboration in schools. *Phi Delta Kappan, 97*(7), 69-73.

Zasa, F. P., & Buganza, T. (2022). Developing a shared vision: Strong teams have the power. *Journal of Business Strategy, 44*(6), 415–425. https://doi.org/10.1108/jbs-04-2022-0065

FIVE

Interprofessional Education Collaborative Pilot: Working Across Disciplines

Patricia Burke

AREAS FOR REFLECTION

- Pedagogical challenges
- Cultural challenges
- Technical challenges

The Context

As participants in a faculty leadership development program, instructors from several of the College's Health Sciences schools were charged with developing and planning a project that would support the mission, vision, value, and strategic plan of the College. Faculty members were from geographically diverse areas, within a large urban metropolitan area in the northeast United States, and the members of the team were from the following schools: dental, osteopathic medicine, physical therapy, and nursing.

The team chose to focus on developing an Interprofessional Education Collaborative (IPEC) pilot program (Interprofessional, 2016). The goal was to embed an interdisciplinary professional health education training model across the many distinct schools and programs that the College offers in the health professions. It was intended that the IPEC would help foster a professional culture; an updated, shared curriculum; and a common perspective that would provide graduates with an authentic skill set and practice with interprofessional collaborative dialogue. The main beneficiaries are the patients that the interdisciplinary teams will care for in the future.

Interprofessional education is defined as students from two or more distinct healthcare professions participating in educational activities together, with the goal of providing patient-centered care (World Health Organization, 2010). These valuable experiences require students and faculty to meet to discuss cases, parallel to what happens in a real-world setting. Additionally, accrediting agencies require meaningful IPE experiences as part of healthcare educational program curricula. The Institute of Medicine (IOM) (2001) recommends interdisciplinary teams to improve patient outcomes. In 2009, six national associations of healthcare formed the Interprofessional Education Collaborative (Interprofessional, 2016). IPEC proposed four essential competencies for IPE: values and ethics, teamwork and team-based care, roles and responsibilities, and interprofessional communication. This is viewed as a necessary step in preparing a "Collaborative Practice Ready" health workforce (World Health Organization, 2010).

At this institution, programs are spread out across a large geographic area, so scheduling in-person meetings is difficult, time consuming, and costly. By using a video conference platform, the IPEC pilot offers the advantage of being technologically based, resource-efficient, and geographically independent, while at the same time enabling the network of health profession programs to advance the College's IPE initiative.

The parameters of the project proposal, provided to participants in the leadership training program, were that the project be developed over eleven months, concluding with a presentation and review by the College's senior leadership. Senior leadership "green-lighted" the project with minor revisions. The team finalized it and began the IPEC pilot within three months. The pilot included the four faculty members who developed the proposal and five students from the dental school. The second phase of the pilot was conducted towards the end of the following semester with three students from each of the four disciplines. Sessions included students and faculty meetings through the video conference platform for a period of 45 minutes to discuss and evaluate each clinical case. Below is an example of a case that was used:

> *A 75-year-old female with a history of hypertension, diabetes, osteoarthritis, peripheral neuropathy, and anxiety. Seen in outpatient dental clinic with chief complaint of jaw pain following a fall, and dry mouth. An interdisciplinary team meeting resulted in a comprehensive plan of care with dental, nursing, and physical therapists.*

Each group described relevant general and profession-specific aspects of the case and collaborated to develop a team management plan of care. Faculty took the role of facilitators rather than lecturers. They were prepared with guided questions and talking points designed to address the IPEC (2016) core competencies for collaborative practice. Students were assigned a pre- and post-session quiz to evaluate their attitudes before and after the activity. Discipline-specific assignments were posted before and after the session (Zorek et al., 2016).

The pilot program was then expanded to include other healthcare disciplines. Under the direction of the dean for Interprofessional Studies, a faculty member from the School of Pharmacy was assigned to coordinate virtual IPE events across the School of Health Sciences, School of Osteopathic Medicine, School of Pharmacy, and the Dental School. Faculty representatives from each school met to develop case studies and domain-specific assignments with three-to-four events scheduled per semester.

Nursing and Occupational Therapy programs developed a joint humanities-based curriculum with a focus on cultural competence. The semester began with a virtual workshop for both groups and wrapped up with a discussion in breakout groups. The teaching/learning strategies utilized included the analysis of a four-part video series on cross-cultural healthcare, as well as a short story. To meet the course learning objectives, the nursing students completed each assignment over the course of six weeks to mirror medical-surgical content. For example, one of the vignettes discussed the cultural perspective of a patient considering renal transplant. Nursing students completed this module a week after studying renal impairment/hemodialysis. The occupational therapy students completed the assignments over a shorter period of time than the other students.

Another outcome of the Master of Science IPE pilot program was the development of a virtual escape room. Faculty from Nursing, the College of Osteopathic Medicine, and the School of Pharmacy developed a case study with three rooms. Students were assigned to interdisciplinary teams and had to work together to escape from each room. Students from each discipline were provided discipline-specific assignments and readings to prepare for the event. Prior to the event, faculty were assigned as facilitators of the student teams. Their tasks were to assign roles within the teams and provide assistance if students had issues. The process required the students to make decisions about patient care with the goal of moving the patient through treatment. After a brief introduction and a review of the instructions, students entered the dental clinic. They then had to answer questions correctly to move to the next "room" to transfer the patient to the emergency department. The third and final room was the medical-surgical floor where the patient received instructions for discharge. Teams had to keep track of the clues to "escape" and successfully discharge the patient. Following the event, the faculty facilitators held a debriefing/reflection session with all the teams sharing the lessons learned.

The Conflict/Challenge

Students participating in the IPE are from different disciplines. They also have different education levels and clinical experiences. There are nursing students in an undergraduate program collaborating with graduate students in professional graduate programs. The IPE experience is to be offered within a course in each program. Nursing courses are taken over four semesters; in the first semester students participate with physical therapy students, learning safe patient handling and mobility techniques. Occupational therapy students address cultural competence in a second semester medical-surgical course. In a level three medical-surgical course, students participate with pharmacy, dental, and Doctor of Osteopathic Medicine (DO) students in virtual simulations for clients with asthma or chronic lung disease. Senior students participate in an innovative escape room with DO and dental students, working in teams to solve a complex, acute case.

Matching the IPE event to meet the course objectives, and scheduling a mutually agreeable time, pose additional challenges. Technology is used to provide a forum for the event. Every program uses the same Learning Management System (LMS). However, lead faculty work closely with the Instructional Design team to coordinate manual enrollment in a separate course that was created specifically for this initiative. There were significant glitches with students' access in the initial pilot.

Questions for Discussion

1. What administrative support is needed to bring multiple professional programs together for an interprofessional experience?

2. What are the best practices to integrate interprofessional education into disciplines other than the health sciences? What would you prioritize to meet the professional standards of multiple disciplines?
3. What are some specific teaching strategies that can enhance the student's learning experience?
4. What are some strategies to expand and sustain an innovative program such as this?
5. Given that students are from different academic levels, different professional cultures, and different levels of practical experience, how should pedagogy be adapted by each school?
6. Given that different disciplines, such as in health sciences, have unique professional cultures, how do you address issues that arise in teamwork?
7. Students have different levels of comfort with technology. When incorporating technologies, such as escape rooms, how are these disparities and how are the various snafus that can occur with technology addressed?
8. How can Interprofessional Education be applied to fields other than the health sciences?

References

Institute of Medicine. (2001). *Crossing the quality chasm: A new health system for the 21st century.* National Academies Press. DOI: 10.17226/10027

Interprofessional Core Competencies. (2016). *Core competencies for collaborative practice.* Interprofessional Education Collaborative. https://www.ipecollaborative.org/ipec-core-competencies

World Health Organization. (2010 , September 1). *Framework for action on interprofessional education & collaborative practice.* https://www.who.int/publications/i/item/framework-for-action-on-interprofessional-education-collaborative-practice

Zorek, J. A., Fike, D. S., Eickhoff, J. C., Engle, J. A., MacLaughlin, E. J., Dominguez, D. G., & Seibert, C. S. (2016). Refinement and validation of the student perceptions of physician-pharmacist interprofessional clinical education instrument. *American Journal of Pharmaceutical Education, 80*(3), 47. doi:10.5688/ajpe80347

SIX

Multidisciplinary Collaborative Leadership for the Infusion of the Collaborative Leadership Curricula[1]

Abraham M. Jeger, Elizabeth J. Unni, and Barbara A. Capozzi

AREAS FOR REFLECTION

- External professional challenges
- Internal mandates
- Professional leadership development
- Leader encouragement of innovation

The Context

The Doctor of Pharmacy programs at all Colleges of Pharmacy in the United States are required to be accredited by the Accreditation Council for Pharmacy Education (ACPE). One of the curriculum standards calls for graduates to be "able to demonstrate responsibility for creating and achieving shared goals, regardless of position" (Accreditation, 2016, p. 2). Furthermore, ACPE stipulates a series of prescribed "co-curricular" requirements in the domains of leadership, communication, self-awareness, and advocacy, among others. These are usually implemented in conjunction with student organization events.

It follows that the American Association of Colleges of Pharmacy (2021), emphasized leadership in its strategic plan. Specifically, Objective 1.1.1 of the plan calls for colleges to "[e]stablish a framework for pharmacy transformation and change that incorporates professional identity formation to help develop a professional mindset and leadership among faculty, learners, and preceptors for an evolving pharmacy workforce" (American Association, 2021, p. 3).

Postdoctoral residency programs are generally accredited by the American Society of Health-System Pharmacists (AHSP). In its statement on professionalism, ASHP includes "leadership" as one of ten salient characteristics of a professional (American Society of Health-System Pharmacists, 2008). It urges all pharmacists, including residents and fellows, to "actively seek the development of leadership skills and exercise leadership when working with others" (American Society of Health-System Pharmacists, 2011, p. 187).

In keeping within this "leadership" spirit, it is no surprise that Touro College of Pharmacy's (TCOP) vision statement calls for "[e]educating and inspiring students to become compassionate, influential pharmacist-practitioners and leaders, who capitalize on their diverse real-world experiences to improve health nationally and globally" (Touro College of Pharmacy, 2022, p. 11). This vision is buttressed by TCOP's strategic plan which calls for the College to become an advocate for the pharmacy profession's expanded scope of practice and to foster students to develop as leaders and innovators.

To address these pervasive calls for leadership education, TCOP's visionary dean, a transformative leader, exploited the potential synergy of several internal leaders (namely, the authors of this chapter) whose professional interests included joining together in the development of collaborative leadership curricula. This chapter captures the essence of how this collaborative leadership across three academicians—trained as a pharmacist, physician, and psychologist—translated into the successful infusion of collaborative leadership curricula along TCOP's Pharmacy Education continuum, including leadership programs for student leaders, PharmD students, pharmacy residents/fellows, and practicing pharmacists. Additionally, in the research domain, a needs assessment survey among practicing pharmacists was used to identify the glaring educational gaps in salient leadership domains, to empirically guide future program development for practicing pharmacists.

It is noteworthy to state at the outset that research and scholarship based on TCOP's initiatives in the leadership area have already been recognized through national academic presentations at the American Association of Colleges of Pharmacy (AACP) annual meetings, as well as other forums. Thus, in keeping with the dictum that good leaders attract loyal followers while great leaders create leaders, the Touro College of Pharmacy (TCOP) is perpetuating its commitment to developing inspiring leaders.

The challenge for this interdisciplinary team was to develop a program for collaborative leadership development where it did not currently exist. In the book entitled, *The Mind of the Leader*, Hougaard and Carter (2018), pointed to a major disconnect on leadership in the workplace, as evidenced by the following findings from extensive survey research:

- 82% of employees felt their leaders were "uninspiring"—even though almost all leaders (86%) thought of themselves as inspiring and good role models; and,
- Only 13% of the global workforce was found to be "engaged," while 24% was found to be "actively disengaged." (p. 2)

Interestingly, the above state of affairs exists, despite the fact that 46 billion dollars is spent annually (at the time of the survey) on leadership development (Hougaard & Carter, 2018, p. 2).

Within the spirit of "thinking globally, and acting locally," our challenge was to create educational prototypes to address this pervasive disconnect. Specifically related to pharmacy, the Association for Health-System Pharmacists' 2012 leadership assessment found that "37% of employers reported that filling a leadership position was more difficult than it was three years ago" (White & Enright, 2013, p. 446).

With the encouragement and unequivocal support of TCOP's dean, a systematic effort was begun in early 2019 to "infuse" a sequential program of leadership development activities along the entire Pharmacy Education continuum. It was to be guided by a framework of collaborative leadership. Each of the activities/programs described in this case study is deemed to be an exemplification of TCOP's response to the previously outlined challenges and mandates.

The team decided that the best way to address the goal of preparing students for leadership in their professional practice was to sequentially infuse leadership development throughout the curriculum. The steps included, among others, are:

Leadership Development Program for Student Leaders: This was initiated in spring 2019, focused on self-awareness and communication skills. It targeted student government officers and officers of student organizations. Faculty was comprised of two of the present authors, Abraham Jeger, PhD, a psychologist and COO/Associate Dean for Student Affairs at TCOP, and Barbara Capozzi, DO, a family physician and Clinical Dean at the Touro College of Osteopathic Medicine-Harlem, NY (New York). Through formal presentations and experiential exercises, the faculty modeled collaborative leadership. These topics were periodically repeated to the larger student body to satisfy "co-curricular" requirements.

Ultimately, this mini-series served as an impetus for proposing the formation of a "Council of Student Organization Leaders." It calls for leadership training of student officers, including an annual leadership retreat.

A New Elective Course, Leadership: Theory & Practice: This is a three-credit course targeting primarily second year pharmacy doctoral students. The development of the course was guided by an overarching framework of collaborative leadership. The salient course goals are to understand one's unique leadership style; develop ethical leadership behaviors; appreciate the role of pharmacists as advocates; develop resilience through self-management skills; apply optimal decision-making strategies; describe major motivation theories and principles; develop professional relationships; foster trust for team-building; and, appreciate the roles of conflict resolution and negotiation to promote individual and organizational effectiveness. Specialized topics include the role of diversity in the pharmacy workplace, unique challenges pertaining to gender relationships, and optimal communication skills for leaders. The inaugural course was offered in the spring 2020 semester and implemented again in the fall 2020, fall 2021, and spring 2023 semesters.

Certificate Program: Leadership for the Frontline Pharmacist: As another first, in January 2020, a pilot certificate program, Leadership for the Frontline Pharmacist, was targeted to a small group of 1199 pharmacy union members. It was organized by the authors, who also served as faculty. As an inter-professional educational team representing psychology, pharmacy, and medicine, we modeled collaborative leadership.

Leadership Certificate Program (LCP) for Pharmacy Residents/Fellows: In the pharmacy profession, leadership positions in health systems, community pharmacies, and industry will most likely be sought after by PharmD graduates who are also residency or fellowship trained (currently only about 15-20% of graduates). Thus, the first two authors developed TCOP's Leadership Certificate Program for Pharmacy Residents/Fellows, which was initially implemented during spring 2021 semester. It was targeted to second-year residents (referred to as PGY-2) and fellows (typically PGY-1) within TCOP's sponsored postdoctoral programs. It is a sequel to the Teaching Certificate Program, geared to PGY-1 residents/fellows. The program was again offered in the spring 2022, fall 2022, and fall 2023 semesters.

The Conflict/Challenge

The authors ask, "Where do we go from here?"

Building on the material in this case, it is our goal to broaden interprofessional collaboration with other Touro University schools and programs such as Medicine, Health Professions, and Business, to name just a few. These might take the form of multi-disciplinary continuing education workshops leading to "micro-credentialing" in a particular leadership domain (e.g., Communication, Trust/Team Building) and/or more substantive certificate programs. Furthermore, our work can provide the impetus to catalyze a degree-granting graduate program in leadership encompassing a common core curriculum, with customized tracks for business, healthcare, and other fields.

Finally, it is our vision that the prototypes described in this chapter will be adapted by schools and programs beyond Touro University, thereby using our work to form the nucleus for potentially broader innovation diffusion.

Questions for Discussion

1. What do you and your colleagues consider to be priority or salient domains of a leadership curriculum for your school/program?
2. What might be required for an infusion strategy to promote buy-in for developing and implementing a leadership curriculum for your school/program?
3. How would you define your constituents or primary targets for a leadership curriculum, (e.g., students, faculty, staff, residents, practitioners)?
4. What challenges or barriers can you anticipate in planning, developing, and implementing a leadership curriculum at your institution? How might you address them?

Note:

1. Acknowledgments: The authors are pleased to express their gratitude to Henry Cohen, Pharm.D., Dean of the Touro College of Pharmacy for his visionary leadership and unwavering support for our work. We are also grateful to Bupendra Shah, Ph.D., Associate Dean of Assessment, and Abigail Bryskin, LCSW-R, Mental Health Counselor/Director of Wellness, Touro College of Pharmacy, for their roles as faculty in various programs described herein.

References

Accreditation Council for Pharmacy Education. (2016). *Accreditation standards and key elements for the Professional Program in Pharmacy leading to the Doctor of Pharmacy degree.* ACPE.

American Association of Colleges of Pharmacy. (2021). *2021-2024 Strategic plan, priorities, goals, and objectives.* AACP.

American Society of Health-System Pharmacists. (2008). ASHP statement on professionalism. *American Journal of Health-System Pharmacy, 65*, 172–174.

American Society of Health-System Pharmacists. (2011). ASHP statement on leadership as a professional obligation. *American Journal of Health-System Pharmacy, 68*, 2293–2295.

Hougaard, R., & Carter, J. (2018). *The mind of the leader: How to lead yourself, your people, and your organization for extraordinary results.* Harvard Business Review Press.

Touro College of Pharmacy. (2022). *2022 – 2024 Catalog.* TCOP.

White S. J., & Enright S. M. (2013). Is there still a pharmacy leadership crisis? A seven-year follow-up assessment. *American Journal of Health-System Pharmacy, 70*(5), 443–447.

SEVEN

Research-Based Learning in the Financial Disciplines—Its Importance and Practical Implications

Anna Klippstein

AREAS FOR REFLECTION

- Interdisciplinary education
- Diverse team/peer group efficiency
- Cross-cultural collaboration

The Context

STUDYING THE FINANCIAL DISCIPLINES PROVIDES students with theoretical knowledge and inspires them to use contemporary digital applications and tools which enable investors to get easy access to the financial markets. In this regard, the practical approach of including workshops, applying case studies, and conducting research projects should become an important part of financial modules within programs leading to degrees in business. Moreover, success in employment and professional life, specifically in the field of finance, is usually tied to newly developed analytical ability and research skills. Young professionals need to be able to follow financial analytics and conduct research independently for smart investment decisions.

In general, education in the 21st century has shifted from "thought" to "doing" (Reimers & Kanter, 2014, p. 4). The Bologna Reform indicated that the quality of higher education should be strengthened by the improvement of research contributions to the process of learning (Empfehlungen, 2008). The innovative strategies of research-based learning are recognized as an improvement in the quality of higher education (Gilardi & Lozza, 2009).

Professor Right from Independent University has started the research project, *Growth versus Value—the Paradigm's Change on the Capital Market.* The goal of the project is to analyze the most successful factors and didactical practices for the finance modules and to exercise reflection and analytical skills. Professor Right has chosen the online format of the project because it enables a combination of different groups of participants—the students of the bachelor's program, the students of the MBA program, and alumni of Independent University (finance business degree)—to work together. These three sample groups represent the University's diversity of competencies, experiences, and skills. The additional component is cultural diversity, as the participants, a total of eight, represent five different countries. The project combines the content of multiple financial courses and aims to guide the participants "from theory to praxis, from knowing to doing" (Huber, 2009).

To share the results of the research project, another digital format of researched learning, a virtual interdisciplinary conference, has been planned by Professor Right. The topic seems to be quite exciting. However, participants were wondering why Professor Right decided to involve the mixed group of participants. The professor believes that the diversity in the group could benefit student learning. The alumni with a financial degree could share with "greenhorn" undergraduate students about their experiences on the capital markets, and actively seek the development of leadership skills and exercise leadership when working with others. The undergraduates would learn to conduct empirical studies while observing the markets and sharing information with MBA students and alumni who have a more mature attitude toward the financial markets. During the workshops and discussions, all participants would create a more in-depth and analytical view of the capital markets.

The task of those in the alumni group would be to share their own investment experience and search for strategies used by various financial institutions based on either value or growth strategies, while the MBA group will have the most analytical part of the project. Each step in the project will be shared and discussed among all the participants, guided by Professor Right. Respecting the need for an interdisciplinary approach, and with the knowledge of different financial disciplines being important to students' understanding of the complexity of capital markets, Professor Right decided to use this collaborative method, gathering MBA students, alumni, and undergraduate students.

The Conflict/Challenge

Despite the perfect planning, a conflict has arisen within the research project team. The experienced alumni, along with the MBA group, are struggling to understand the role of undergraduate students in the project. Given the time pressure faced by the alumni and MBA students due to their work, family responsibilities, and academic commitments, they are hesitant to assume an "educational function" for the undergraduates.

Questions for Discussion

1. What oversights or misjudgments did Professor Right make during the project planning phase that contributed to this conflict?
2. How might Professor Right have proactively addressed potential conflicts within the research team while still maintaining the involvement of undergraduate students in the project?
3. If you were in Professor Right's position, what strategies would you employ to help undergraduate students grasp the concepts of financial markets and understand the practical implications of financial studies?
4. Would switching from an online format of the project to an in-person format potentially facilitate better collaboration within and among the groups, and if so, how?
5. What could Professor Right do to assuage the concerns of the MBA and alumni members of the group?

References

Empfehlungen zur Qualitätsverbesserung von lehre und studium. (2008). *Wissenschaftsrat.* https://www.wissenschaftsrat.de/download/archiv/8639-08.pdf?__blob=publicationFile&v=1

Gilardi, S., & Lozza, E. (2009). Inquiry-based learning and undergraduates' professional identity development: Assessment of a field research-based course. *Innovative Higher Education, 34*(4) 245-256.

Huber, L. (2009). Warum forschendes lernen nötig und möglich is. *Förschendes Lernen im Studium: Aktuelle Konzepte und Erfahrungen, 10*, 9–35 Bielefeld: UniversitätsVerlagWebler.

Reimers, F. M., & Kanter, R. M. (2014). *Harvard Education for 21st Century Executive Summary.* Harvard Advanced Leadership Initiative. https://globaled.gse.harvard.edu/files/geii/files/2014_education_report_web.pdf

EIGHT

Faculty Leadership in Professional Communities of Practice

Elina Lampert-Shepel, Marcella Bullmaster-Day, and Laurie Wellner

AREAS FOR REFLECTION

- Leading program quality improvement
- Building a culture of collaboration
- Developing faculty as leaders

The Context

Riverview University, located in a large Northeastern metropolitan area, enrolls approximately 2,300 master's degree candidates annually in programs that lead to initial teacher certification. Because these programs are so large, multiple class sections of each course are offered each academic term, fall, spring, and summer. Courses are offered in three formats: asynchronously online; synchronous video conference; and in-person class meetings. Therefore, as many as 14 different instructors, full-time and adjunct, teach sections of the same course each academic year.

To ensure consistency and comparable quality of degree candidates' learning experiences, and to provide opportunities for instructors to collaborate on course design, the program chair, working with the associate dean of Academic Affairs, initiated the establishment of Course Teams ten years ago. The goal was to build professional Communities of Practice (CoPs), ensuring faculty ownership of co-designed course content as they continuously engaged in sharing resources, discussing concepts taught in the courses, and investigating problems of practice and successful learning strategies. From these collaborative interchanges, shared course syllabi are improved from term to term, and faculty best practices are shared across all sections. Through this collaborative process, courses evolve as outcomes of faculty teamwork rather than through top-down or as inherited products.

The Riverview Course Team model of the CoP is grounded in social constructivist theory as applied to learning and leadership (Lambert et al., 2002;

Warhurst, 2008) and grows from the belief that ongoing reflection and dialogic inquiry among a group of instructors can strengthen their teaching and their students' learning. The nexus of these transactional relationships is Vygotsky's (1978, p. 32) "zone of proximal development:" the distance between a learner's current level of unassisted individual understanding and performance and the level they can reach with the help of people, tools, and powerful artifacts (Brown, 1994; Tharp & Gallimore, 1988).

The goal is that Course Team participation will transform the culture of isolation prevailing in academia to a culture of collaboration among instructors. Meaningful learning in the social context of Course Teams requires the interplay between participation and reification. As Course Team participants move from peripheral participation to leading the discussion and contributing to course development, they acquire self-efficacy and ownership of course content and methods, value the joy of professional collaboration, and reflect on their own professional growth. By participating in Course Teams as CoPs, teacher educators learn across the multiplicity of practices that shape their growth in practice and encourage them to pass on the value of inquiry to their teacher candidates.

Under the facilitation of a Course Team leader, instructors integrate three elements: a shared domain of interest, community participation, and practice (Wenger, 1998). They value their collective competence, learning from one another and building community by engaging in joint activities and discussions. They collaboratively generate a shared repertoire of resources—experiences, stories, tools, approaches to solving recurring problems—that is, a shared practice.

The program chair recognized that to effectively develop Course Teams as CoPs, several conditions needed to be fostered. These include a shared practical task (course design and implementation); safety and trust; openness and respect; collaboration and ownership; challenge and empowerment; and creativity and enjoyment.

Infusing trust into the Course Teams as CoPs requires the group to organically engage in the building of relationships, collaboration, dependence, and cross-team expertise with leadership from the Course Team leader. Intentional community-building strategies such as encouraging open communication and fostering collaboration on shared goals (Barnett & Carroll, 2015) support trust-building across faculty, with most faculty developing trust over time. These experiences over the ten years have demonstrated the value of the contributions and voices of all members by validating diverse contributions for the multiple sections of the same course. This has promoted increased reliance on the collaborative process to achieve consistency through the shared professional and academic practice of creating a meaningful and relevant product.

Many students come to class, whether virtual or onsite, with a varied history of preparation in the field of education. Therefore, Course Team leaders initiate the use of a "Teaching Memo" to function as a meditational means (Wertsch, 1998) of communication between the instructor and the student for added clarification of content, to clear up misunderstandings, and to apply real-life situations to the students' application of the content in their day-to-day employment. At the conclusion of each asynchronous course module, or after a class meeting, the instructor posts a re-cap of vital points from the assigned readings, videos, and class discussions.

The Teaching Memo brings consistency in content implementation and provides an opportunity to share student comments, questions, course reminders, and upcoming due dates. The preparation and use of the Teaching Memo continue to serve as a leveling tool for instructive purposes and to bring consistency to all students, given their varied backgrounds and experiences. Through the implementation of Teaching Memos, positive, high-impact feedback continues to operate as a critical component of the learning process, especially that which is meaningful, relevant, and directly aligned to the content.

The Conflict/Challenge

Establishing and sustaining these Course Teams as professional CoPs faced several challenges. To maintain consistency and quality, it was vital that all instructors follow the same syllabus, course structure, and content as posted on the Learning Management System (LMS). Instructor buy-in was essential, even though new instructors were assigned to work with what the team from the previous semester had designed and then to participate in further work to improve the course.

Many instructors had previously been teaching their own versions of a given course. Initiating this change required instructors to move from a mindset of working alone to that of engaging in the collaborative process of course improvement and ensuring consistent learning experiences for degree candidates, regardless of which instructor they were assigned. Further, adjunct instructors comprise the majority of most of the Course Teams, so this resulted in challenges in coordinating logistics around schedules and meeting times.

Over the ten-year period, these faculty Course Teams developed through different approaches. Initially, teams organically formed under the program chair's leadership. The chair participated in all teams, facilitating learning and development. As programs expanded, seasoned Course Team leaders naturally emerged to guide the Course Team transformation.

More recently, the program chair acquired two additional programs lacking a history of Course Teams as CoPs. With urgent curriculum revisions needed, the Course Team leaders were appointed administratively rather than emerging through their participation and group interactions. This change risked teams' perception of leaders as those wielding power versus those who are facilitators based on their abilities and influence. This adjustment required a re-envisioning of team development to ensure future collaboration and support.

Questions for Discussion

1. In what ways does your institution implement and sustain professional Communities of Practice?
2. In traditional academic settings where "academic freedom" is frequently invoked to protect faculty from being required to cooperate in group efforts around course improvement, what are the tools that foster inquiry, discussion, and collaboration in course design in service of high-quality learning and teaching while building trust within your teams?
3. When rapid program growth requires appointing team leaders, how do you prepare the team leader? How do you motivate other faculty members to accept this person who did not emerge organically as the team leader?
4. How might a new team develop into a Community of Practice or other high-functioning team?

References

Barnett, K., & Carroll, G. (2015). Forming the teaching team. *The Department Chair, 26*(1), 23–25. https://doi.org/10.1002/dch.30047

Brown, A. L. (1994). The advancement of learning. *Educational Researcher, 23*(8), 4–12.

Lambert, L., Walker, D., Zimmerman, D. E, Cooper, J. E., Lambert, M. D., Gardener, M. E., Szabo, M. (2002). *The constructivist leader*. Teachers College Press.

Tharp, R. G., & Gallimore, R. (1988). *Rousing minds to life: Teaching, learning, and schooling in social context*. Cambridge University Press

Vygotsky, L. (1978). Interaction between learning and development. *Readings on the Development of Children, 23*(3), 34–41.

Warhurst, R. (2008). 'Cigars on the flight deck': New lecturers' participatory learning within workplace communities of practice. *Studies in Higher Education, 33*(4), 453–467.

Wenger, E. (1998). *Communities of practice: Learning, meaning, and identity*. Cambridge University Press.

Wertsch, J. (1998). *Mind as action*. Oxford University Press.

NINE

Organization or Chaos? Kicking Off an NGO

Shamira Malekar

AREAS FOR REFLECTION

- Communication barriers
- Decision-making processes
- Balancing diversity and goals

The Context

THE GLOBAL FEDERATION (TGF) SOUNDED like a great idea. Most individuals joining were in India and Israel, though members were also in the United States, United Kingdom, Australia, Canada, and the African continent.

The enthusiasm of the organizers showed in their Facebook posts about what TGF would be:

- "How I wish the younger generation could help seniors across the world connect with each other."
- "The senior citizens' wishing bell continues to ring."
- "Let's draft an agenda for our meetings that goes beyond meet-and-greet and [honors more than] a select few."
- "I want to build a long-term sustaining model to help the community rather than make a glorified 'kitty' party."

The underlying belief of TGF was that there was a need for a long-term sustaining model to assist the community. Their idea was that youth should take charge of protecting and sustaining the future of customs, traditions, and heritage. As many interests were represented in TGF, there were numerous objectives driving its leaders towards accomplishing the organizational goals. These interests included:

a. Formalizing and registering the organization, which would legitimize it and facilitate stronger backing and financial support.
b. Providing encouragement and pride for youth to maintain their cultural identities.
c. Assisting those in the communities to secure jobs where needed.
d. Creating housing for senior citizens immigrating from other countries and helping young people find jobs.
e. Ensuring senior citizens are taken care of and not left alone.
f. Safeguarding the possession and control of community landmarks.

TGF was to be organized as an NGO (Non-Governmental Organization) with the expectation that the designation would help facilitate funding to support the goals and related planned activities. NGOs are non-profit organizations that are independent of government influence, although they may receive government funding. NGOs are formed to further a social or humanitarian mission, and their activities can include advocacy, service provision, capacity building, and public education (United, 2024).

A committee was formed to plan an introductory event to launch and publicize the new NGO. It included members from several nations, and some members, but not all, were senior citizens. This first organizing meeting was in Mumbai, India in January, with virtual participation from around the world. It was decided that the first annual gathering would be also held in Mumbai, on the 14th of January the following year. This in-person event would publicly launch the new initiative. The committee decided to communicate largely through group messages on WhatsApp.

However, as the year progressed, challenges arose. Lack of planning, communication barriers due to virtual teams being situated in different countries with different time zones, mismanagement, and financial pressures contributed to the problems. In an effort to be inclusive, the committee gave more weight to the suggestions of members residing outside India. Because an awards presentation ceremony was planned for only a select few, the choice of the awardees led to a feeling of animosity and resentment among the committee members. Also, because the event had to satisfy all interested parties, it was scheduled with a great many speeches, but some members advocated for a shorter ceremony. Additionally, building consensus around the date of the event had been difficult.

For the NGOs first public event, it was decided to have a designated group visit a historic cemetery in Nagaon, a suburban town in the state of Maharashtra, India, wherein tombs of the first settlers of the community are located. As the story goes, owing to a storm at sea, the group was shipwrecked, and only seven males and seven females survived. The total population grew from those seven couples.

A meet-and-greet was scheduled as part of the agenda for the first public event. To align with the historic setting, traditional food items from the past were considered to be a requirement but caused multiple complications. With so many hands involved, the event started to look like a glorified women's social event at home, commonly called a *kitty party* in India. Despite the difficulties, the event was held, and it was well received. Additionally, registering as an NGO was critical and involved documentation. This was not done until December, only a month before the event.

The Conflict/Challenge

After the event, new complications came to light. With the lack of organization, some committee members were overreaching in an apparent desire to help. For example, a college professor in New Jersey found that another committee member, a prominent woman from the Middle East, had committed him to pay for the cost of the event programs. It was widely known that the professor knew publishers in India, which led to the assumption by the woman that the cost of publishing the programs would be borne by the professor. Compounding her error, she did not solicit a quotation for the cost of publishing the event programs.

The professor came to know about his sponsorship in April, long after the event in January. When he reviewed the balance sheet that included Assets and Donations on WhatsApp, he saw his name associated with an uncollected donation amount. All of this was after the programs were published. The professor had never even received a copy.

The second annual community gathering was cancelled. Organizers claimed that the cancellation was due to the event conflicting with national elections in two major world democracies.

Questions for Discussion

1. What went wrong?
2. How did the multiplicity of goals of TGF undermine its success? Do you find this issue in higher education?
3. What strategies could a university use to plan and execute an international conference or event?
4. How would you organize a committee representing diverse cultural perspectives and still accomplish the organization's goals?
5. What is the optimum size of a committee for an event such as this?

Reference

United Nations Development Programme. (2024). *Nongovernmental organizations.* https://popp.undp.org/taxonomy/term/6216

PART II

DIVERSITY, EQUITY, AND INCLUSION

TEN

Getting Students to Focus on Feedback Rather Than Grades

Charity Dacey

AREAS FOR REFLECTION

- Establishing effective feedback strategies
- Supervisory responsibility
- Faculty-student relationships
- Balancing compassion and adhering to standards

The Context

THE TEACHER PREPARATION PROGRAM IS in the mid-Atlantic region of the United States. The program chairperson has formed course teams of professors that meet three times a term to discuss course implementation and student grading issues. These teams are largely autonomous and are only loosely supervised by the chairperson. Instructors on the team collaboratively examine grade distributions from the prior term, unpack feedback strategies, and problematize grade disputes. They also compare different assessment philosophies and debate the advantages of implementing different grading models: a) grading relative to independent standards of performance; b) grading relative to peers; or c) grading relative to individual potential, effort, or past performance (Reich, 2002).

Dr. Harding is a diligent and popular adjunct professor who teaches each semester for the teacher preparation program. Dr. Harding taught high school biology for eight years in a large urban high school. She spent her first-year teaching special education science at a public charter school, where she learned to differentiate instruction to meet the diverse learning needs of her students. At the university, she serves as the course team leader, guiding instructors teaching the introductory assessment course to both pre-service and practicing teachers. Based on candidates' performance on a newly developed end-of-program portfolio performance assessment, the course team of instructors has been grappling with the implications for improvement to the assessment course. Results show a need to increase pre-service teachers' long-term learning and development for their students. The results also indicate that students need exposure to culturally sustaining practices, and strategies to foster equity, inclusion, and accountability (Paris & Alim, 2017).

The Conflict/Challenge

Recently, Dr. Harding has been mentoring Mr. Schwartz, a new adjunct professor on the teacher preparation program course team. Mr. Schwartz reaches out to her via email because he has several pre-service teachers who are struggling to pass his class. He tells Dr. Harding that he believes in the importance of providing his pre-service teachers with extensive feedback so that they can improve their work, and upon graduation and certification be able to better serve their PK-12 students. He tells Dr. Harding that he is distressed by the pushback he receives from the pre-service students, some of whom disregard his feedback. He relates that he has even experienced some who complain about being asked to revise and resubmit assignments. Mr. Schwartz goes on to state that based on what he is told by some students, and his own discussions with colleagues, he has learned that some professors give full credit for unfinished papers or assignments turned in late, despite the university grading policies. Mr. Schwartz is concerned about holding students accountable: "We are not grading uniformly here at the University, and I do not want my course evaluations to suffer because I am not as lenient as other professors."

Dr. Harding and Mr. Schwartz decide to meet. In the meeting they agree about the value of providing actionable feedback to support student growth. They also recognize that in this large program there is a variety of opinions about grading, and this is often discussed at the course team meetings. They have observed that there is a clear division about the issues of professor responsibility and the personal work ethics of the pre-service teachers. They end their meeting on this note, agreeing to see each other at the next broader course team meeting.

Because a review of grading practices was a charge given to the team by the chairperson, Dr. Harding decides to bring the subject of grading practices up again during a course team meeting. While Dr. Harding and Mr. Schwartz attempt to get their colleagues to share their viewpoints about the provision of actionable feedback and the allowance of multiple revisions, they are met with fierce opposition from a number of colleagues. Some instructors argue that they have large course loads and that allowing revisions is an imposition on their time. Others argue that the students need to take ownership of their own growth and that if they do shoddy work, they should not pass. Still, others believe that leniency in grading should be provided to some students who otherwise will never be able to pass their courses and complete the program. At this point, Dr. Harding determines that she is not her colleagues' supervisor and that the program chairperson should address this conflict.

Questions for Discussion

1. What leadership traits does Dr. Harding exhibit in listening and responding to her mentee, Mr. Schwartz?
2. What should the chairperson do upon hearing about this conflict?
3. What responsibilities does a leader have to ensure consistency in grading in a program?
4. What is your opinion about a chairperson delegating programmatic decisions to course teams?
5. How do you balance adhering to standards and being compassionate?

References

Paris, D., & Alim, H. S. (Eds.). (2017). *Culturally sustaining pedagogies: Teaching and learning for justice in a changing world.* Teachers College Press.

Reich, R. (2002) *Bridging liberalism and multiculturalism in American education.* University of Chicago Press.

ELEVEN

Job Interviews Analysis Overstep?

Lenin Ortega

AREAS FOR REFLECTION

- HR procedures
- Discrimination in hiring
- Uniformed Services Employment and Reemployment Rights Act

The Context

WHEN AN ADMINISTRATIVE SUPPORT STAFF member in a health-related academic program resigned from the University, a vacancy was created. The job posting included the following requirements: applicants must be detail oriented, proactive, computer literate, knowledgeable about ordering medical supplies, and available to work on Sundays. The position also requires the applicant to be self-motivated, proactive, and work unsupervised in a remote environment. After the position was posted, numerous resumes were received.

A search committee with four members, including the supervisor, reviewed dozens of resumes and identified three individuals to move to the interview stage. The supervisor decided to interview the three individuals, without the other committee members present, and bring the most well-suited individual to the rest of the committee for a final decision. All three candidates were interviewed on the same day:

- The first candidate had no work experience; the interview took about 20 minutes.
- The second candidate had work experience and some skills related to administrative support, but not in a health-related academic environment. The interview lasted about 20 minutes.
- The third candidate had work experience in a health-related field, but not in an academic environment. The work experiences this candidate had aligned closely with the job description. The interview lasted about 33 minutes because the supervisor asked many follow-up questions.

All the candidates interviewed were asked about Sunday availability. The first and second candidates were available to work on Sunday. The third candidate said she was available most Sundays; however, she is a military reservist and will have to use one weekend every month to fulfill requirements with the United States Army.

The supervisor wrote his analysis of each candidate to share with the rest of the search committee. The first candidate was rejected due to the lack of experience. The second candidate was rejected due to the lack of experience in a health-related field. The third candidate was rejected with the following statement: "There is the issue of release time, as she is still in the reserves. Because the program is running on skeleton staff, this will be an issue. She is an excellent candidate for an entry-level administrative position in another department."

The Conflict/Challenge

After the email was sent to the search committee, one member, who is a veteran replied, "There is no issue about release time!!! Military personnel and reservists are protected by the federal government when they receive orders for training." The committee member requested that the third candidate be offered the position.

The remaining search committee members met through video conference and made the decision to consult the Human Resources department. Human Resources concluded that the third candidate should be recommended for the position to reduce the perception of discrimination. The supervisor was highly upset, feeling that he was being forced to hire the third candidate.

Questions for Discussion

1. If you were the supervisor in this situation, how would you handle the interview and selection process?
2. What is the supervisor's responsibility so he can avoid discrimination before making an offer?
3. As a committee member, what responsibility do you have to question the search process, as it was implemented?

4. What other unrecognized biases have you observed that possibly violate anti-discrimination laws?
5. How could the Human Resources department have been more definitive in the advice given the supervisor?

TWELVE

Addressing Evolving Historical Perspectives[1]

Alan Sebel

AREAS FOR REFLECTION

- Difficult conversations
- Cultural sensitivity
- Preserving history vs. contemporary perspective
- Balancing perspectives

The Context

PORTNOY UNIVERSITY, NESTLED IN THE heartland of the United States, proudly bears the name of Henry Portnoy, the intrepid explorer who played a significant role in the early exploration of the American frontier. The University's campus boasts a magnificent mural in its lobby, depicting Portnoy alongside Native Americans, symbolizing the historical encounter between European explorers and Indigenous communities. However, recent demands from descendants of the Native American Nations depicted in the mural have sparked a contentious debate: Should the mural be removed? This case study explores the complex challenges faced by the University's leadership.

Henry Portnoy is a celebrated figure in American history. He explored the central and western territories of the continent from 1790 to 1820. His excursions are viewed to be as important as those of Lewis and Clark. The large mural, created by a renowned artist, captures the moment when Portnoy encountered Indigenous peoples on the frontier of what is now the state of Utah. It celebrates cultural exchange, but it also reflects the power dynamics and complexities of colonization. The Native American descendants argue that the mural perpetuates a Eurocentric narrative and fails to acknowledge the painful legacy of colonization. They demand that the mural be taken down to create a more inclusive and respectful environment.

Native American students and faculty assert that the mural occupies a central space in the University, a space that should be reclaimed to celebrate their own heritage and stories. Administration believes that the mural serves as a historical artifact, representing the era of exploration and cross-cultural encounters. Removing it might erase an essential part of America's past.

The Conflict/Challenge

The University's leaders are faced with a challenge that threatens to tear the University community apart. They see the need to balance the celebration of Portnoy's achievements with acknowledging the pain and suffering experienced by Native Americans during the westward expansion of the United States. The controversy has attracted media attention and threatens the University's reputation. The leadership must navigate this delicate situation while maintaining transparency and sensitivity.

At the same time, the leaders must balance the viewpoints of multiple stakeholder groups. These include the University administration who are responsible for making a decision that aligns with the institution's values and mission; the Native American representatives advocating for cultural sensitivity and the removal of the mural; faculty and students, both with Native American roots, and non-Native American heritage who have divergent positions on whether the mural should be removed; and the general public who are observing how the University addresses the challenge.

Given this divergent and controversial set of options, the leadership ponders several options:

- Retain the mural and acknowledge its historical significance while providing additional context to promote understanding.
- Modify the mural in collaboration with Native American artists to add layers of meaning or incorporate Native American perspectives.
- Remove the mural, which will address the concerns raised by the Native Americans but risk backlash from other stakeholders.
- Change the name of the University to one without cultural or historical relevance.

The leadership of Portnoy University faces a formidable task—balancing respect for history, cultural sensitivity, and the well-being of their community. Whatever decision they make will shape the University's identity and its commitment to reconciliation and inclusivity.

Questions for Discussion

1. The leaders consider holding a "town hall" to allow the differing perspectives of the issue to be voiced. What might the possible outcome be of holding this "town hall"?
2. As the leaders consider the four options, how can they ensure that their ultimate choice will be acceptable to the broadest group of stakeholders?
3. What additional solutions might the University consider to resolve this controversy?
4. If the University decides to remove the mural, what ramifications could arise?
5. If the University decides to keep the original mural, what might the ramifications be?
6. How should the University's leadership address public relations controversies to ensure the least damage to the institution?

Note:

1. This case was generated by Microsoft Copilot AI with prompts provided by the editor. AI provided the foundation of the case and the editor refined the content.

THIRTEEN

Introducing Critical Race Theory[1]

Alan Sebel

AREAS FOR REFLECTION

- Difficult conversations
- Leading change
- Managing conflict

The Context

The undergraduate Economics Department at Smytheton College is a leader in the field. The department's mission is to provide students with a comprehensive and inclusive education. The school has a student body and faculty that is mostly white, with a strong commitment to social justice and equity.

Critical race theory (CRT) is a theoretical framework that examines the ways in which race and racism intersect with other forms of oppression, such as class, gender, and sexuality. CRT has gained increasing attention in recent years as a means of understanding and addressing systemic inequalities in education.

The chairperson of the undergraduate Economics Department proposes that the faculty redesign an economics course to include a thread on critical race theory. The course will replace an existing course for students pursuing a degree in economics. The chairperson believes that the course will provide students with a deeper understanding of the ways in which race and racism impact the economy.

Some faculty members are in favor of the proposal, arguing that CRT is an important framework for understanding systemic inequalities. Without understanding the historical, legal, and institutional factors that contribute to disparities, present-day challenges cannot be fully addressed. The proponents believe that the course will provide students with valuable knowledge and skills that they can apply in their future careers. They argue that a common criticism of CRT is that it is divisive and inaccurate; however, they believe that learning about CRT promotes critical thinking and reflection.

Some faculty members have presented arguments against teaching CRT. The faculty members who oppose the proposal argue that CRT is divisive and promotes a victim mentality. They believe that the course could be detrimental to students' learning experiences. Their position is that if faculty members are perceived as strongly advocating for or against CRT, it may lead to a perception of bias in the classroom or might instigate emotionally charged discussions. As a result, this can create tension between students and faculty, or among students, thereby hindering open dialog and constructive learning experiences.

The Conflict/Challenge

The split between faculty members in both "camps" has created tension within the department. Some faculty members have expressed frustration with what they perceive as a lack of open dialogue and understanding among colleagues. Others have expressed concern about the potential impact of the split on student learning experiences.

Key factors contributing to the split include differences in ideological perspectives, individual experiences with racism, and perceptions of the relevance of CRT to economics.

Analysis of underlying reasons for faculty members' positions reveals deeper ideological differences related to issues such as race, power, and privilege. These differences reflect broader societal debates about social justice, equity, and diversity.

The tension has also spilled over onto student experiences. Some students have reported feeling uncomfortable or unwelcome in classes where discussions about CRT have taken place. Others have expressed frustration with what they perceive as a lack of clarity about how CRT relates to their future careers in economics.

The potential consequences for student learning and engagement are significant. If faculty members are unable to bridge their differences and create a more inclusive learning environment, students may miss out on valuable opportunities for growth and development.

Questions for Discussion

1. How can leaders in higher education foster open dialogue and understanding among faculty members with differing perspectives on issues related to diversity, equity, and inclusion?
2. What strategies can be employed to address tensions among faculty members related to issues such as race, power, and privilege?
3. How can higher education institutions ensure that discussions about controversial topics such as CRT are conducted respectfully and productively?
4. What role do professional development opportunities play in promoting diversity, equity, and inclusion within institutions of higher education?
5. How can leaders in higher education balance competing demands related to academic freedom, intellectual diversity, and social responsibility?
6. What are some strategies for fostering a more inclusive environment in the classroom?

For Further Reading

Delgado, R., & Stefancic, J. (2017). *Critical race theory: An introduction* (3rd ed.). New York University Press.

Ladson-Billings, G., & Tate IV, W.F. (1995). Toward a critical race theory of education. *Teachers College Record, 97*(1), 47–68.

Note:

1. This case was generated by Bing AI (Artificial Intelligence) with prompts provided by the editor. AI provided the foundation of the case, and the editor refined the content.

FOURTEEN

Rhetoric and Practice

Velma Cobb

For we have, built into all of us, old blueprints of expectation and response, old structures of oppression, and these must be altered at the same time as we alter the living conditions which are a result of those structures.

—*Audre Lorde*

AREAS FOR REFLECTION

- Equity in practice
- The language of equity
- Being neutral (playing it safe) vs. advocacy
- Communication of institutional conscience

The Context

Hancock University is a mid-sized higher education institution on the East Coast, where a rich history of public and private higher education institutions, both large and small, exists. Hancock is a private University with a conservative religious foundation. As is the case in many higher education institutions, following the COVID-19 pandemic, most programs are now offered in a variety of formats: asynchronous, through video conference, and onsite. Also, like many institutions, the national social unrest that occurred simultaneously with the shutdown precipitated institutional reflection at Hancock, leading to the release of a diversity statement acknowledging the United States' persistent and ongoing inequities. The statement covered the usual federal designations of race, gender, natural origin, and religion. However, it also included the evolving terminology of cultural identity and LGBTQ+ to include queer, transgender, non-binary, etc. The statement was not out of character for Hancock. "In the service of knowledge, community, and social justice" begins the University's Mission Statement:

Hancock University believes in the humanity of all people and is committed to the values of social justice and equity for all. The university works towards building

> racial consciousness and fluency across our institution. Hancock creates spaces of dialogue and learning around issues of race, context, and systemic racism to build a more inclusive and equitable environment for students, faculty, and staff. Hancock is dedicated to promoting equity and excellence in the education of the professions and overcoming the gaps in multi-disciplinary fields to garner access and achievement between the most and least advantaged groups in this country. Through programs of teaching, research, and service, the university draws upon the expertise of a diverse community of faculty in psychology, education, and health, as well as students and staff from across the country and around the world.

The Graduate School of Psychology and Applied Health Sciences operates the Wilson Center for People, Practice, & Context, envisioned by Hancock's founder and first president Frederick R. Wilson. Dr. Miranda Collins is the current director of the center. Under Collins' leadership, the Wilson Center supports various state and federal grants and sponsors professional development programs for both faculty and students. The Wilson Center sponsors Faculty Brown Bags where faculty share their research and professional expertise, and it also offers the PPC (People, Practice, & Context) series, including outside speakers presenting on practice and emerging educational issues.

Programs are held monthly. Although some programs have been offered in person, increasingly, programs are offered virtually, via video conference technologies. The speaker series is intended to bring to the campus thought leaders in a range of fields to promote contrasting ideas and emerging research. Typically, the posted schedule of programs includes a flyer with a brief written blurb about the program and a photo and bio of the presenter or presenters. As each program date draws near, a markup of the flyer goes to the Graphics and Communications Office to finalize advertising for the event with registration instructions. Though the dean is aware of all programs, Collins is given the leeway to invite guests she deems appropriate. Collins identifies as Pacific Islander, and it just so happens the current dean is of Asian descent. Collins was hired long before the sitting dean.

Generally, the identification of speakers is through faculty suggestions and contacts or presenters encountered at professional conferences. The Wilson Center has a very lean budget for these programs, so only a very small honorarium is paid to invited speakers.

The Conflict/Challenge

As the program for the fall semester begins to take shape, Collins is particularly excited that Dr. Taylor Lee-Jones has agreed to do the program for December. Lee-Jones is a West Coast educator whose research focuses on adolescent development. She has developed a "Framework for Flourishing." Her research especially focuses on LGBTQ+ students. Taylor Lee-Jones is a renowned researcher in the area of youth development and a much requested speaker, and she has agreed to waive her usual fee. Collins views this program as a real benefit because the speaker series rarely secures well-known educators due to the Center's budget constraints.

Collins sends the bio sent by Lee-Jones as is, along with the program blurb, and registration link to the Graphics and Communications Office. The bio is submitted as follows:

> Dr. Taylor Lee-Jones is the Director of Education Programs and Research for the American Justice Coalition (AJC). In this capacity, Dr. Lee-Jones is responsible for leading AJC's efforts to ensure that policy, practice, and praxis account for the diverse experiences of, and unique contributions made by, trans, queer, and non-binary youth, both in and out of schools, and people in society, more generally. She manages the Flourishing Campaign; she is also establishing the organization's research agenda and is helping to position AJC as a global leader in research, thought, and cultural competence development toward advancing radically-inclusive social justice. Taylor's mission is to increase possibilities for thriving among those who experience complex marginalization. Her particular focus at the intersections of age **x** sexuality **x** gender **x** race **x** ability is grounded in the knowledge that design driven by those (currently) furthest from power improves all our lives. Through her scholarship, Dr. Lee-Jones has developed an intersectional Framework for Flourishing, which she uses with activists, educators, scholars, youth, and others to advance the shared project of building universal thriving.

Shortly after submitting the mark-up, Collins is contacted by the senior vice president for Academic Affairs. Though no direct comments are made, it becomes clear that the bio submitted was considered problematic. Collins rightfully registers that she is being asked to reword the bio. No mention is made regarding the program blurb. Collins makes the changes directly to the bio without input from Lee-Jones. The following bio is accepted.

> Dr. Taylor Lee-Jones is the Director of Education Programs and Research for the American Justice Coalition (AJC). She manages the Flourishing Campaign; is establishing the organization's research agenda; and is helping to position AJC as a global leader in research, thought, and cultural competence development. Dr. Lee-Jones has distinguished herself as a thought leader and collaborator in the worlds of youth service, education, mental health, well-being, and social justice research. Through decades of work across communities, non-profits, universities, K12 schools, think tanks, and foundations, she has developed a deep understanding of how to support young people, teams, and organizations. Taylor's mission is to increase possibilities for thriving among those who experience complex marginalization. Through her scholarship, Dr. Lee-Jones has developed an intersectional Framework for Flourishing, which she uses with educators, youth, and others to advance the shared project of building universal thriving.

With these changes to the bio, the program is approved.

Collins is torn regarding the implied request to take words—*trans, queer, and non-binary youth*—out of Lee-Jones's bio. The direct language that spoke to the complex nature of intersectional identities and the subsequent marginalization of certain populations was a way of recognizing and inviting those in the University's community to identify with the stories of other youth. It also acknowledges the scope of identities among the college's varied students. Derald Wing Sue (2013) discusses the avoidant behavior of majority cultures. When the naming of the range of identities is avoided, marginalized communities can see these omissions as microaggressions that negate one's identity. When Collins pushes back somewhat, she quickly learns the entire presence of the Wilson Center is under inquiry, and discussions have begun about reorganizing the center.

Questions for Discussion

1. How might the invited speaker react to her bio being revised?
2. In light of the fact that no direct language was used to ask Collins to redo the bio, can this be called an equity issue?
3. How might the inquiry into the Wilson Center be interpreted?

4. Because the senior vice president for Academic Affairs contacted Collins directly, why might the current dean have not played a larger role in this situation?
5. What might be concluded about Hancock University relative to its Mission and the Diversity Statement and practice on the ground? What might be the perception?
6. While the University's Mission Statement is worded to be inclusive, how might the institutional climate in practice reveal a different feeling for traditionally marginalized groups working and enrolled in the university?

References

Lorde, A. (2007). Age, race, class, and sex: Women redefining difference. In A. Lorde & C. Clarke, (Eds.), *Sister outsider: Essays and speeches*, (pp. 114–123.). Crossing.

Sue, D. W. (2013). Race talk: The psychology of racial dialogues. *American Psychologist, 68*(8), 663.

FIFTEEN

The Team Leaders' Dilemma

Ruth A. Best

AREAS FOR REFLECTION

- Human Resources processes
- Investigate before you advocate
- Personnel management

The Context

A Fortune 100 company has an Operations Management Department with a hierarchical top-down management style. This department has been experiencing several conflicts. Ms. Foley, a newly appointed middle manager within the organization, has multiple departmental teams reporting to her. Mr. Ashford, the operations team leader, reports to Ms. Foley, and has been with the organization for five years. He has an open-door policy and holds weekly check-in meetings with his operations team.

Mr. Ashford and his line staff work in different locations. In line with the company's policies regarding attendance, workload, and time on task/on-site, the organization established rules for off-site workers. Anticipating that staff would comply with these guidelines, there was a significant amount of trust assumed. In accordance with labor law, the staff were allowed two 15-minute breaks and an hour lunch during a typical 8-hour workday. There was a set policy that one of the staff should always cover each department. This was done to maintain good customer service so that someone was always available to assist clients. Recently, however, there were complaints from clients about the staff not responding to emails or phone calls promptly. Also, employees from other departments complained about the staff missing deadlines. One day, while walking around during lunch, Mr. Ashford observed that none of the staff that reported to him were on post, so he decided to alert middle management.

There were several violations of trust and conflicts brewing within the department. For example, recently, after receiving a poor performance evaluation, one employee reported her supervisor to Human Resources. The outcome of the conversation and investigation by Human Resources resulted in the female supervisor being relieved of her managerial position.

From this point on, some staff felt emboldened to get their supervisor "in trouble" by making reports to middle management, senior leadership, and Human Resources personnel. Mr. Ashford's staff began to slowly challenge his authority by refusing to follow directions. When they should have been productive and on task, they were chit-chatting with members from other teams. They took long lunches with other team members without consulting or alerting Mr. Ashford. In essence, they became recalcitrant and stopped following directions. They joined a group of other staff who were dissatisfied with their salaries and filed a petition that was submitted to Human Resources. Ironically, during this same time, Mr. Ashford had been advocating to Ms. Foley for a merit increase in salaries for all the staff on the Operations team.

In confidence, while seeking advice on how to address some of the emerging personnel issues, Mr. Ashford shared his concerns with Mr. Wong, a manager from the Purchasing department. Little did he know that his colleague would tell Mr. Golden, a disgruntled staff member on Mr. Ashford's Operations team.

The tale involved Mr. Golden's direct supervisor, Mr. Ashford. Rather than approaching Mr. Ashford to discuss what he had heard, Mr. Golden shared the rumor with his colleagues. It was well known that Mr. Golden did not like taking directions from Mr. Ashford, who was of a different ethnicity and religion than he was, resulting in a breakdown in communication and trust between them. This not only affected Mr. Golden's relationship with Mr. Ashford, but also impacted the overall department culture.

A few of Mr. Ashford's team members approached his supervisor, Ms. Foley, to report him. Two of those staff members were resentful because they were on improvement plans due to their chronic lateness, long lunches, and limited productivity. This impacted the functioning of the busy department. As the story continued to circulate and grow, none of his colleagues from other departments thought to apprise Mr. Ashford of the backdoor conversations or find out the truth about the story.

Previously, the word among the different department teams was that they envied the relationship and openness evident among Mr. Ashford's Operations team members. However, it seemed that since Ms. Foley came on board, Mr. Ashford noticed a change in the staff's behavior and sensed a change in their interactions with him. Yet he was unaware of the cause and rumors floating around. Thus, the surprise and sense of betrayal when the team finally decided to approach him to share their concerns.

The Conflict/Challenge

Rather than speaking to all parties to fully understand the situation, when approached by Mr. Ashford's staff who were complaining about him, their salaries, and other concerns, Ms. Foley sent out an email to all team leads and supervisors, stating that one of them had committed a specific infraction. Rather than discussing the issue with Mr. Ashford and redirecting the staff directly to him, Ms. Foley decided to act based on hearsay—a one-sided account that fueled the rumor mill.

Mr. Ashford was in shock and numb upon learning through the grapevine that his staff members had reported him, and that he was the person to whom Ms. Foley was referring. He felt betrayed by Ms. Foley who, after a month in this role, obviously was working hard to be accepted in her new work environment. This would become one of many instances where Ms. Foley would show poor judgment and not seek out evidence prior to sending out email communications to direct reports. The people who reported to her often perceived this type of communication as offensive, disrespectful, and non-collegial. This behavior resulted in a suffocating toxic environment for some; others appeared oblivious while trying to please Ms. Foley. Mr. Ashford was stunned that the team members he had mentored with extensive training and development opportunities were the ones who would betray him.

Questions for Discussion

1. Considering what you know about the principles of management and leadership, what is happening, and why?
2. Who is at fault, and why?
3. Putting yourself in the role of each of the players, how would you respond, and why?
4. How do ethics play out in this case study?

5. What impact can a situation like the one presented in the case have on employee morale?
6. Is it ethical to go to another leader in the organization for advice? Why/why not?
7. What are best practices around establishing trust with and between people of different ethnicities, religions, and races?
8. What is the solution to this dilemma?
9. How would you restore trust, open lines of communication, and enhance the corporate culture? Why did you choose what you did?
10. If you are a leader in a higher education setting, what could you take away from it to avoid similar issues?

For Further Reading

Abiodun, A. J., & Oyeniyi, J. O. (2011). Ethical Dilemmas in Management. *Journal of Law and Governance*, 6(2), 39–48.

SIXTEEN

"This Is Not a Game Any Longer!" Opportunities and Challenges of Advancing Applied Studies by Introducing Computer Simulations

Holger Luedeke

AREAS FOR REFLECTION

- Applied learning
- Interdisciplinary pedagogy
- Diversity, equity, and inclusion

The Context

Professor De Huis couldn't believe it. Not even three weeks had passed in this new semester, and he was already facing more problems in his newly designed management course than in all his other courses put together.

Everything had looked so perfect in theory. His University, with its small classes, interactive learning concepts, and focus on excellence in teaching, was tailor-made for a stronger focus on applied teaching. Professor De Huis was particularly proud of recruiting students from non-subject areas such as psychology and the healthcare professions for this simulation. The business simulation was designed for a general management class, mainly necessary for business majors; however, the opportunity to manage their own business was at least as relevant for others as it was for business students.

In how many pedagogical training courses had he heard about the enthusiasm of the students when more opportunities for real-life applications were incorporated into the lessons? After all, it was particularly interesting and motivating for the students to have the challenge of engaging in practical business tasks in an authentic context (Baldwin et al., 2011). Not only that, but numerous studies also promised above-average progress in learning (Luedeke & Brock, 2023).

Professor De Huis had incorporated two of the most successful concepts for greater application focus into his new management course. First, the entire course was based on a *computer simulation* that students were asked to play every week. The learning goal for this is clear: Web-based management simulations are defined as "[i]nternet-based, synthetic learning environments where decisions are made within a complex and dynamic setting, and where students experience real-time information and feedback" (Lovelace et al., 2016, p. 101).

The simulation used by De Huis had the usual design of such games: Student teams had to make a series of decisions in an environment that replicates a typical workplace. De Huis designed the semester so that, during each week, the students working in groups made investment decisions and entered them into the simulator. The simulator gave them immediate consequences about the success of their decisions, representing the passage of three months. The course would be completed in one semester, yet the virtual experience would span three years in the life of the business. Feedback included how their decisions affected sales, brand reputation, and employee motivation within their company in the game. Unlike many other classes based on theoretical lectures, students would learn by trial and error and by pragmatic correction of the errors revealed through fast feedback from the simulator.

Now, in the third week of the game, students had already chosen their teams and their company brand. They had made business decisions twice, covering six months of the game that would last three (virtual) years overall, ending in the last week of the semester.

For the midterm exam, each group of students would have to defend its previous management decisions in a presentation. Professor De Huis had built in a second application component here: He required a *role play* for this presentation, in which the students would have to dress and behave like real managers. Accordingly, he had invited some acquaintances with a management background to comprise an audience to ask the students questions as conversation partners in the role play. At the end of the semester, this was to be repeated in a second role play in which the students were to present and defend their results.

The role play also had a clearly defined educational objective: In experiential role plays, students are exposed to critical business incidents, and they are also supposed to re-live the troubling cognitive limits of corporate decision-making and even the emotions involved in difficult discussions, simulating a "direct, personal encounter with the phenomena being investigated" (McCarthy & McCarthy, 2006, p. 201). Role-playing allows for practicing behavioral guidelines repeatedly in an academic, low-risk environment, and for adapting the theoretical principles to personal style through repetition and learning from feedback (Whetten & Cameron, 2015).

Another positive impact on students is from meeting actual practitioners and learning about business details that cannot be found in textbooks. This allows for "knowledge-by-exemplification: one that is demonstrative, creative, and unreflectively performative, transmitted directly through the demeanor, style, and mannerism of management educators rather than through the content of lectures" (Chia & Holt, 2008, p. 471). The underlying pedagogical concept is that many ways of operating in business are forms of tacit, practical knowing that can be learned only through participation and imitation of experienced business experts (Chia & Holt, 2008).

With this innovative pedagogical concept, business simulations combined with role plays, Professor De Huis felt well prepared for a successful course experience. And this is when the trouble started.

The Conflict/Challenge

Incident 1: Avoidance of Technical Management Skills.

In the very first week, the teams had to establish themselves as the management of various fictitious companies. Their initial decisions included group formation and the division of specialist responsibilities. This meant that the students should have decided on a functional specialization, (that is, appoint one person to be responsible for marketing, one for production, another for financing, etc.). This was not only to simulate the typical company management with its CFOs, COOs, CMOs, and others, but also to strive for actual advantages through specialization. The students were told that their grading would also be based on specialization, (for example, the CFO would be graded on the quality of financial policy).

While this happened in some groups without further ado, two of the teams immediately experienced fundamental "teething" problems. First, the participants refused to be tied down to specializations. Instead, all upcoming questions were to be decided in group discussions. Second, the groups complained of disadvantages compared to their more specialized competitors. After all, not specializing means significantly more time spent on decision-making and less differentiated results.

As the professor's inquiries revealed, the problem was the participants' lack of self-confidence, as the majority of them studied outside the management subjects. Management was only an additional qualification for these students of psychology, health sciences, and education.

Professor De Huis was not sure how to solve this. On the one hand, these students actually lacked the basics in technical skills such as accounting, market research, or corporate finance, which were needed in the simulation. Also, the participants should not have been scared off by excessive requirements of learning about concepts outside their specialty areas, as Professor De Huis saw the future of his University as creating synergies across management, psychology, and medical programs.

On the other hand, these non-specialist students were much more likely to have to perform management tasks in a health practice or in an independent capacity in their later professional lives. In addition, the simulation had a glossary in which every key financial figure and every business statistic was explained simply and in detail. It was not for nothing that well-known management consultancies such as McKinsey had crash courses set up for their new recruits outside the business administration specializations, in which the entire methodological knowledge of the management sciences was taught within a few months. The methodological knowledge was catchy and easy to understand and apply. So, what stopped students from learning it?

Incident 2: Avoidance of Role Plays.

Another surprise awaited Professor De Huis in the unexpected total rejection of the pedagogical concept by a small group of students. On the one hand, they declared that they were not prepared to pay the basic fee for participating in the simulation. Instead, they preferred to participate as unpaid advisers to other students who had already paid for access to the simulation. They also rejected the idea of role-playing, perceiving it to be "childish" and "ridiculous." Instead, they wanted to present advice without appearing to be managers.

Only when the professor asked more detailed questions did it emerge that the group of objectors were students from socially disadvantaged families. Granted, the game fee was too expensive for them; but they also felt they were at a disadvantage in management role-playing games compared to other students who were already able to demonstrate the kind of management behavior expected in role-playing games through their parents' professional and business-oriented households. For other students, the roles felt inauthentic and contrived.

Again, Professor De Huis was undecided. Indeed, in traditional lectures there are easy ways for students to save on educational investment, for example by borrowing textbooks from the library. Simulations, however, require the individual registration of participants. It is not only necessary to respect the property rights of the publishers, but also, obtaining detailed individual feedback for decisions is possible only if each participant is registered individually. Unfortunately, the dean had already expressed his unwillingness to provide additional funding for simulations. The program's desire to avoid costs was understandable. Yet, this means disadvantaged students will gain less feedback and less learning experience from the simulation.

As for not using role-plays, Professor De Huis understood the desire to put the substance of the decisions above the superficiality of the presentation style. He realized that students from business- and management-oriented families arrived in his class with some advantages when it came to understanding some of the business functions and the meaning of professionalism; he also knew that these students and those coming from less business-oriented backgrounds would benefit from socializing and working with one another. Study after study in management research has shown that self-presentation and self-confident role behavior are more likely to be the deciding factors when it comes to graduates getting the best-paid entry-level jobs—more important than particularly good grades or particularly good factual knowledge (Rivera, 2016). And self-confident role behavior can be learned relatively effectively in management skills training, in using exercises such as role plays (Whetten & Cameron, 2015).

Professor De Huis was at a loss. He would never have dreamed that a simulation game would challenge not only the students but also himself so much.

The Conflict/Challenge

How could the conflict surrounding the use of the simulation game be addressed, considering that students from other specializations often try to avoid technical subjects like finance or accounting that are essential for every realistic start-up? What could the solution be? A reorganization of the teams to better mix management students and students studying within other fields? Some extra training for the non-specialist students? Or simply lower expectations for students from disciplines outside the field of management?

Does applied business education offer unfair advantages to students with a family background in business and management? Should role plays be voluntary, as they can be overwhelming in a complex and dynamic simulation with numerous decisions required? Or does the decision to make role plays voluntary create and/or amplify a much more significant bias against family backgrounds in which business and management role models do not exist, thus causing the gap in soft skills (for example, professional relationship-building, presenting to peers and superiors) will continue? Is it justified to create additional challenges for less business-oriented families, or would it be better to require role-playing games separately in other courses (such as Human Resources Management)?

Questions for Discussion

1. What are the advantages and disadvantages of a stronger focus on applied learning in higher education?
2. Should different standards be used for students from different disciplines when they must demonstrate their management skills in practical exercises?
3. What can be done to deal with the basic problem of privilege—students with relevant backgrounds, including family modeling and mentoring, having a head start when it comes to knowing what to do in professional and business-related situations?

References

Baldwin, T. T., Pierce, J. R., Joines, R. C., & Farouk, S. (2011). The elusiveness of applied management knowledge: A critical challenge for management educators. *Academy of Management Learning & Education, 10*(4), 583–605.

Chia, R., & Holt, R. (2008). The nature of knowledge in business schools. *Academy of Management Learning & Education, 7*(4), 471–486.

Lovelace, K. J., Eggers, F., & Dyck, L. R. (2016). I do and I understand: Assessing the utility of web-based management simulations to develop critical thinking skills. *Academy of Management Learning & Education, 15*(1), 100–121.

Luedeke, H., & Brock, S. (2023). Does business familiarity breed liking or critical distance? The impact of applied business education on social evaluations of firms. In B. Wold, T. Schmohl, L. Buhin, & M. Stricker (Eds.), *From splendid isolation to global engagement: Exploring internationalization in higher education*. wbv Media GmbH & Company KG.

McCarthy, P. R., & McCarthy, H. M. (2006). When case studies are not enough: Integrating experiential learning into business curricula. *Journal of Education for Business, 81*(4), 201–204.

Rivera, L.A. (2016). *Pedigree: How elite students get elite jobs.* Princeton University Press.

Whetten, D. A., & Cameron, K. S. (2015). *Developing management skills.* Pearson Education.

SEVENTEEN

Inclusive Realities of a Virtual Campus: Navigating Accessibility Changes in Virtual Learning Environments

Ayushi Tandon

AREAS FOR REFLECTION

- Balancing fiscal considerations and accessibility
- Defining empathetic project management
- Considering accessibility evolution
- Anticipating management questions

The Context

In the rapidly evolving landscape of virtual reality (VR) education, Studia, an immersive learning start-up, faced a pivotal challenge in ensuring inclusivity within its VR campus. Partnering with the View Group, a subsidiary of Forecast Reality, the collaborative venture sought to address accessibility issues reported by users. These challenges encompassed a spectrum of concerns raised by the users of their VR campus having such characteristics as color blindness and limb differences, highlighting the pressing need for accommodations within the virtual environment. This case study unfolds the journey of creating accessible VR environments and introduces the empathetic VR development process. As the Studia and Forecast Reality teams grapple with these challenges, the narrative sheds light on the importance of early expert involvement, continuous inclusivity testing, simulated disabilities during development, and the iterative process through to quality assurance testing. The context underscores the broader implications for the future of VR in education and the necessity for a nuanced, empathetic approach to education technology development, resonating with the increasing drive for accessible virtual learning experiences.

Embarking on the journey to enhance accessibility within Studia's VR platform started with a meticulous process rooted in empathy and user-centricity. The initial step involved thorough research, reaching out to individuals with diverse accessibility needs and hence various technological needs. Through insightful interactions, the team gained a deep understanding of common struggles, laying the groundwork for a more inclusive design. Rigorous review of accessibility standards, such as Meta's (2024) VRCs (Virtual Reality Check) and Web Accessibility Guidelines (WAG), guided the identification of specific requirements for immediate focus and those slated for the future roadmap.

Recognizing the importance of a step-by-step approach, a dedicated team of designers, developers, and a project manager collaborated to create a comprehensive development timeline and collaborative working methods. Drawing inspiration from existing accessible apps in the app store, the team compiled a pro/con list, learning valuable lessons to inform their design choices.

Throughout the design phase, the team prioritized creating solutions that would enhance usability for a broad user base. The process involved diagnosing and addressing individual areas of inaccessibility, with detailed documentation outlining the requirements and reasoning behind each redesign. Forward-thinking guidelines for future accessible design were crafted, ensuring an iterative approach aligned with user feedback. Utilizing tools such as Figma for quick mockups and ShapesXR for spatial and interactive prototypes, the team brought their design concepts to life. Regular communication with users ensured feasibility and alignment with design tenets. Taking cues from non-VR apps, the team navigated the development phase with user reviews to assess progress and seamlessly integrate features into the platform. Post-development, the team conducted quality testing with users having special needs and simulated disabilities. This included users within Studia's user base. The iterative nature of testing and implementation revealed the importance of flexibility toward user needs in the product roadmap, where basic features served as a foundation for subsequent improvements.

This holistic approach is a comprehensive five-step process outlined in the outer circle of Conrad et al.'s (2021) framework (Fig.17.1). The Forecast Reality team's design journey emphasizes the value of empathy, collaboration, and continuous improvement, such that Studia's VR platform evolved to

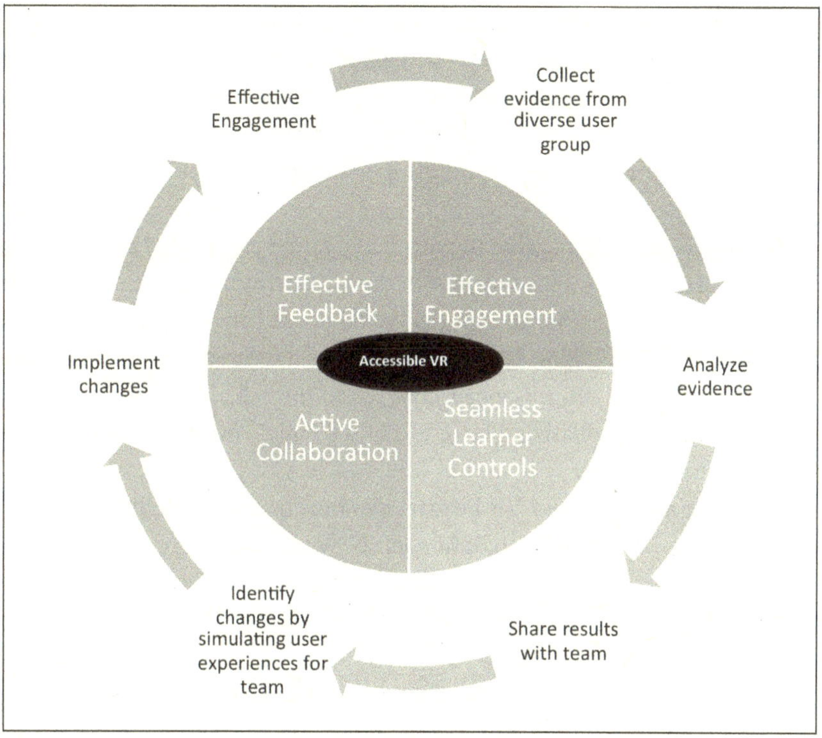

Figure 17.1. Framework for teaching case: VR accessibility.

provide an accessible and enriching experience for many users with special needs. But this is an ongoing process.

The Conflict/Challenge

Excitement turned to frustration for Ryan, a user navigating Studia's VR environment. Unclear icons hindered his exploration, prompting the need for self-explanatory symbols or informative tooltips to ensure inclusivity. In a similar session, Emily, a user with visual impairments, desired the Studia campus to provide her with a seamless experience that blends haptic and audio cues. The existing disconnect in the current campus design highlighted the importance of synchronized sensory channels. This emphasized the need for incorporating the expectations of visually impaired users while planning features of immersive experience. Another participant, John, while navigating the VR space, struggled with the legibility of menu text. Error messages in red on a white background posed readability challenges. John's experience underscored the importance of adequate contrast levels and adjustments for color blindness accessibility, prompting the team to rethink color schemes and streamline text.

Nitisha, a user with hearing impairments, found closed captioning essential for understanding conversations in the VR environment. The team made changes and called on her to experience the revised environment. However, the initial implementation had flaws—captions appeared over her head and caused discomfort. Nitisha's experience led to the refinement of closed captioning features, emphasizing large text and strategic overlay positioning for improved accessibility.

Naveen, unable to use a VR headset due to migraines, sought an alternative. The absence of a desktop option left Naveen excluded from the immersive experience. This incident prompted the team to incorporate a desktop version, ensuring accessibility for users like Naveen and maintaining consistency with the VR counterpart.

Uncovering these issues provided pivotal moments driving the team to prioritize accessibility considerations and refine the VR environment. In preparation to meet with the owner of Studia, the team outlined the steps and the additional budget needed to continue to refine the VR platform. However, when the budget was presented to the owner, he peppered the development team with questions: "This whole process costs way too much money. Furthermore, the projected timelines mean we will not meet our primary client's deadlines. You need to go back to the drawing board immediately."

Frustrated, the design team decided to put off considering their boss's objections until the next morning.

Questions for Discussion

1. Can advanced multimedia features coexist with accessible design in virtual learning environments, or is compromise crucial?
2. What are the legal considerations regarding accessibility in the design of emerging technological environments?

3. How does this relate to higher education as leaders develop new programs and use new technologies?
4. In what ways does the continuous commitment to accessibility testing demonstrated showcase a genuinely empathetic project management style in VR development?
5. In the realm of VR, what strategies employed by Forecast Reality and Studia offer valuable insights for you to lead the development of inclusive and accessible design for emerging technologies?
6. What is the best strategy for the design team in addressing their boss's objections?
7. What could the team have done differently to avoid this conflict?

References

Bureau of Internet Accessibility. (2023). *Website Accessibility Audits (WCAG 2.1 AA).* https://www.boia.org/accessibility-services-for-digital-compliance/accessibility-audits/website-accessibility-audit

Conrad, M., Watkins, L., & Singmaster, H. (2021). A framework for global social justice in CTE. *Techniques: Connecting Education and Careers, 96*(4). https://www.acteonline.org/tech-global-social-justice/

Meta. (2024). *Meta quest virtual reality check (VRC) guidelines.* https://developer.oculus.com/resources/publish-quest-req/

PART III

FACULTY-ADMINISTRATOR RELATIONSHIPS

EIGHTEEN

Administrative Integrity vs. An Organization's Policy

Thomas Troisi

AREAS FOR REFLECTION

- Faculty-administrator relationships
- Policy vs. practice
- Administrative discretion

The Context

THE SETTING FOR THE FOLLOWING case study is a small but very selective liberal arts college in Ohio. Anthropology is among the College's several curriculum offerings. The Anthropology Department is administered by a chair who also teaches a reduced course load. There are also six full-time faculty members. As with most "middle-level" management positions, the duties of the department chair are diverse but people-centered. Within the chair role, a considerable amount of time is spent on personnel management. Most of the time, the faculty issues managed by the chair tend to be routine, such as handling issues related to payroll and scheduling classes for the semester. Less often, issues may arise that truly test the leadership skills and ethical resolve of the chair. In those rare cases, more formal and legalistic decision-making may be required. This is "rare" because, in that smaller subset of instances, the decisions one makes may result in the formal discipline of a faculty member. Understandably, during those times, the chair may feel intense pressure, as loyalties to faculty and upper-level administration are necessarily stretched. That is one reason why it is incumbent for the head of an academic department to understand and fairly administer the faculty agreement with the institution. At the college to be discussed, the faculty agreement contains the following language: "*A faculty member may be disciplined or dismissed for a variety of reasons including incompetence, dishonesty, theft or misuse of college property, and acts of discrimination*," as well as several other causes. It is against this contractual language that the reader must weigh the facts of the case. This case study examines and applies significant leadership-related issues such as policy vs. practice, faculty/administrator relationships, and administrative discretion.

Rebecca is an Associate Professor of Anthropology at the College, which is a tenure-granting institution. She has been teaching at the College for more than a decade and has consistently received positive reviews from her students. During that period, Rebecca was granted two semester-long paid medical leaves of absence by the board of trustees to receive treatment for breast cancer. She is not the first member of her department to have battled cancer, and she has received a considerable degree of support from her chairperson, Melissa, along with her other colleagues.

Midway through Rebecca's second medical leave, Melissa called Rebecca at home to address a matter of departmental business. Rebecca's teenage daughter, Lena, answered the phone call and explained that her mother was out of the country and was uncertain of her return date. Additionally, Lena was unaware that her mother had taken a medical leave of absence and appeared confused by Melissa's questions regarding the present state of Rebecca's health.

One week later, Rebecca resurfaced in Ohio and returned her chairperson's phone call. Melissa requested that Rebecca meet with her to discuss what appeared to be some confusion regarding the Associate Professor's health status. During that meeting, Rebecca confided in Melissa that she did not have breast cancer and had used each of her medical leaves for overseas travel. She further explained that she needed to travel out of the country twice to secure loans from a relative. Rebecca sobbed as she explained how her husband, a registered pharmacist, had serious legal problems that stemmed from his alleged unlawful sale of opioid drugs. As a result of his actions, he not only lost his license to practice pharmacy but also was required to pay fines totaling more than $300,000. Rebecca also explained that she was not, at present, living with her husband, as he had recently become verbally and physically abusive. She pleaded with Melissa not to reveal her situation to anyone at the College.

Following her meeting with Rebecca, Melissa was visibly shaken. She had known Rebecca for several years, and as the department chair, had strongly recommended her for tenure. Additionally, Melissa had been an outspoken critic of relationship violence both on and off campus. As both a colleague and a woman, she was more than sympathetic to Rebecca's domestic strife and feared for her safety. However, at the same time, she began to question the veracity of Rebecca's recent admission, for if she had lied about having breast cancer, might she be lying about her reasons for having left the country, twice?

Melissa also considered those other faculty members who had truly been stricken by cancer. What would their reactions be if they were to become aware of Rebecca's most recent revelations? Melissa began to experience the "push and pull" in her allegiances as the leader of an academic department. As much as she wanted to protect a colleague and friend, her ethical conscience and moral compass provided a "tap on her shoulder." Despite Melissa's sympathies for Rebecca, would she remain silent regarding what might be considered a significant personal matter? Didn't Rebecca, for certain, mislead or deceive the board of trustees about the reason for her two semester-long leave requests?

Melissa's responsibilities as a leader drove her to gather more information before making any decision. As she read through the College's faculty agreement, Melissa readily found her way to the section related to faculty discipline. She noted the passage that began with the words: "*A faculty member may be disciplined or dismissed for a variety of reasons including incompetence, dishonesty, theft or misuse of College property, and acts of discrimination,*" as well as several other causes.

The Conflict/Challenge

Melissa's dilemma illustrates one of the many kinds of internal struggles that are often experienced by competent department leaders. As a leader, Melissa cares a great deal about each member of the Anthropology Department. She has listened to and counseled several members through serious illness and other life crises. They, in turn, generally respect her authority as a leader, and they also respect her judgment. Yet, there are times—rare ones, it is hoped—when the department chair must also weigh the integrity and good of her department and the College against the rights or actions of an individual member. Of course, the easiest thing to do would be to do nothing. Perhaps if Rebecca returned to work next semester, no one else would be the wiser. After all, did Melissa not have a moral obligation to maintain her colleague's privacy? If what Rebecca told her was true, should she not try to help her?

But what about Melissa's obligation to the College and the other members of the faculty? Also, to cover Rebecca's classes, the College had created a visiting professor's position during her absence. If Melissa were to reveal Rebecca's secret to the dean, there could very well be profound consequences ranging from a letter of reprimand to termination.

Questions for Discussion

1. What are the several factors that Melissa should consider before making any decision regarding Rebecca's standing at the College?
2. What do you think are some of the potential risks associated with Melissa's doing nothing about what Rebecca has revealed?
3. What do you think are some of the potential risks associated with Melissa reporting what she has learned to the dean of the College?
4. If you were Rebecca's department chair, what decision would you make? What would be the rationale for your decision?

NINETEEN

Planning the Unplannable

Gena Bardwell, Carrie DiMatteo, and Sabra Brock

AREAS FOR REFLECTION

- Dialogue between front-line staff and administrators
- Improving relevance of required meetings
- Modifying last-minute planning behavior
- Intervening in personality conflicts
- Technology assists to teaching soft skills

The Context

A COMPREHENSIVE PROGRAM FOR DEVELOPING FRONT-LINE staff skills in empathy had been something that Meals for Children (MC) had wanted to start for many years. The not-for-profit had been founded in the 1980s when the AIDS crisis left many children without a functioning adult in the household to prepare meals. The staff who delivered the meals daily had been encountering problems beyond the need for healthy nutrition for the family, but there was no training in how these serious issues were handled or reported. It was believed that training in empathy toward clients in general and for the most common issues reported needed to be provided for front-line staff.

The Meals for Children structure had six vice presidents overseeing the operational departments, which included food preparation, client vetting, social services, technology, and budgeting, as well as food delivery. There were several hundred full-time people in delivery positions, divided into groups of approximately 50 based on geography. An additional part-time staff of equal size was employed seasonally.

The supervisors of the five groups reported to Administrative Vice President Arista. Melody Arista was one of the founders of Meals for Children. Her assistant Carl Cunningham was an up-and-coming newcomer with a master's degree in social work. He liked to think he was "heir apparent" for the VP position when Vice President Arista would retire later in the year. Carl was tasked with creating the Empathy Prompts app to be used by the delivery staff. He relied heavily on the program developed by the Meals for Children Social Services Division headed by Dr. Herman Paz.

Several months of work went into building an empathy assistance program and installing the app on handheld devices that each delivery staff member carried. The background of the delivery staff was varied, with no universal hiring qualification other than a high school diploma. Staff members were also required to have health and criminal clearances. It helped to be comfortable with technology, so new hires tended to be younger, with the ability to use the handheld devices which came with little instruction.

The twice-a-year organization-wide meeting of delivery workers seemed to be a good place to start the training for using the Empathy Prompts app. These meetings had been held for decades, and the organization calendar always carved out a specific day each year for this meeting, when deliveries could be made the night before so that meal delivery would not suffer. Each year, this was called Skills Day. Full-time delivery staff were required to attend, and it was highly recommended for part-timers to attend. Typical programs opened with a report from each of the vice presidents and program heads as to the success and issues from their perspectives in the current season. A theme was selected, and a keynote speaker followed the "parade of vice presidents" that opened the meeting. This was followed by a morning of speakers with expertise on the theme subject, in this case "Responding Empathetically to Clients."

Food was considered key to getting delivery staff to attend. A continental breakfast was served, and lunch was included. Typically, at least 100 people would attend.

The afternoon sessions were organized into smaller groups and centered on a specific skill, such as how to handle client issues requiring an empathetic response. These could range from getting food and care for household pets to notifications from schools when children had to stay home to care for parents. Each session would be led by a delivery staff member and usually involved a working session. There would also be a review and practice on efficient and effective use of handheld devices.

The Conflict/Challenge

The program for Skills Day had been planned by a faculty committee, but Vice President Arista usually specified a focus. This time she wanted to concentrate on getting delivery staff to upscale their empathy skills.

There was an underlying personality conflict between Vice President Arista and the man who had founded and managed the Social Services Department, Dr. Herman Paz. Open conflicts had previously been reported between them in the meetings of senior staff. Dr. Paz was a strong leader, and he appeared to have plans to take over the Delivery Services vice president position when it became vacant. His Master of Science in Social Work and Doctorate in Business Administration in Project Management would lend credibility to his qualification for the position. Furthermore, he and Carl Cunningham, who also hoped to replace Vice President Arista upon her retirement, had been involved in several disputes.

The Skills Day committee had five members. The Committee Chair, Anna Zayman, a star in the organization, was rumored to be on her way to a Regional Section Leader position. Working out the details of the program was left to the committee.

Anna reached out to Dr. Paz, who was delighted to be asked to deliver the keynote speech and viewed it as a platform to publicize the empathy training program. He proposed that after he gave the keynote speech, his staff would facilitate workshops with small groups of attendees from each regional department, with the objective to train delivery workers using the Empathy Prompts app on the new handheld device that each carried. He would provide a canned presentation of PowerPoint slides that each session leader would use.

At the last minute, unfortunately, the Social Services Department staffers were not available to help with the sessions due to the inability to compensate them through a budget transfer. At least that was the stated reason; however, the general buzz in the office was that this reflected the underlying personality conflict between Vice President Arista and Dr. Paz. The Skills Day committee would have to provide the essential help for delivery staff expected to learn how to use the Empathy Prompts app and apply the online tools at the point of delivery. The date for Skills Day was set with no date change possible, and Dr. Paz was still committed to delivering the keynote. Anna pondered how the day could be saved and what the committee could do to prevent such a dilemma in future Skills Day events.

Questions for Discussion

1. How could the committee keep the structure of the day in place without the help of Dr. Paz's facilitators?
2. What role might a mid-level committee play in moderating personality conflicts between their leaders? Should they even try?
3. What provision should the committee make for discovering and documenting the success/failure of the upcoming Skills Day?
4. How would you evaluate the professional behavior of Vice President Arista and Dr. Paz?
5. What lessons can higher education take from not-for-profit organizations which need to train large groups of professionals in new technologies?

TWENTY

Procedural Disfunction

Alan Sebel

AREAS FOR REFLECTION

- Ethics and professionalism
- Procedural clarity
- Leadership discretion

The Context

Alpina University is a mid-sized private university in the central United States. The University offers programs at the undergraduate, graduate, and doctoral levels in a variety of disciplines including business, education, the health sciences, engineering, medicine, and law, among others. At the graduate level, one of the largest schools is the School of Business. The Graduate School of Business has several programs including Public Health Administration, Government Services, and other majors related to commercial business leadership. The Public Health Administration program is led by a chairperson and includes three full-time faculty and two adjunct faculty.

In January, at the start of the spring semester, one of the senior public health administration faculty members informed the chairperson that he will be retiring at the end of the semester. The chairperson informs the dean of the Graduate School of Business. Following the University's hiring procedures, the dean tells the chairperson to prepare an advertisement for the position and to establish a committee to review the applications, set up interviews, and make a recommendation about the best candidate to fill the vacancy. It is the policy of the University that the chairperson of a department can be on the search committee, but not head the search committee. The chairperson of the Government Services program has been asked to lead the search committee. The committee will also include the chairperson of the Public Health Administration program and two full-time faculty members, one from the Public Health Administration program and one from the Government Services program. After the application date has passed, the committee meets to review the applicants and determine who will be called for an interview. The committee decides to interview seven applicants, five external applicants with no relationship to Alpina University and two adjunct faculty members.

It is now late spring, and the dean would like the decision made by July 1st so that the new hire will be able to start work for the fall semester. The interviews begin, and one of the outside candidates seems well-suited to the position. Yet there is nothing significant to distinguish her from the two adjunct faculty who are also applicants and similarly qualified. In her interview, she lets it be known that she has a prior professional relationship with the dean.

She worked at a hospital as an administrator in the same county as the university where the dean worked. They knew each other, as the hospital regularly served as a site for health administration interns who were supervised by the dean. One of the faculty members on the committee decided to do an Internet search of the remaining applicants before the committee sent a list of finalists, in rank order of preference, to the dean. As was University policy, the dean would then send the list of finalists to the provost who would make the final decision.

The Internet search resulted in some distressing information about the applicant. It indicated she was fired from the hospital for apparent misdirection of funds. The articles in the local newspapers uncovered that she had also been dismissed from a previous position for similar actions. The committee member brought this information to the committee. The committee determined not to forward the applicant's name to the dean and recommended that one of the adjunct faculty be hired. The committee chair hand-delivered the list to the dean.

The Conflict/Challenge

When the dean saw the list, he inquired about the applicant that he knew from his previous position. The committee chair told him what was discovered through the Internet search. She stated that the committee believed, strongly, that this person was not representative of an ethical businessperson and would not be an appropriate role model for students. She further argued that if the applicant was hired and a student happened to conduct their own Internet search and found the same information, it would be embarrassing to the University. The dean ordered the committee chairperson to add the applicant to the list as the "number one" candidate for the position. The committee chair refused. She then informed the other committee members.

Questions for Discussion

1. What steps should the committee take next?
2. Why or why was it not appropriate to conduct an Internet search for background information on the applicants?
3. From an ethical standpoint, who acted in an ethical manner in this case, and why do you believe this to be true?
4. From an ethical standpoint, who acted in an unethical manner, and why do you believe this to be the case?
5. If the demands of the dean are reported to the provost, what do you think the provost should do?

TWENTY-ONE

Trouble Due to Pilot Error

Timothy Bellavia

AREAS FOR REFLECTION

- Internal and external demands
- Faculty engagement
- Faculty development
- Addressing student needs

The Context

Departments of Education in several states chose to mandate that educator preparation programs (EPPs) use a newly developed teacher performance assessment for candidates who are not yet certified to teach (pre-service teachers). The assessment is performance-based and is designed to determine a pre-service teacher's ability to plan, implement, and assess effective instruction through 15 tasks. Pre-service teachers use a digital portfolio to provide evidence of their ability to meet the requirements of the assessment. Trained scorers from an external assessment developer use a rubric to assess the pre-service teachers' performance on each task.

One state adopted the teacher performance assessment without providing some universities adequate time to prepare either the candidates or the instructors to become familiar with the rigorous demands of the new test. Due to this lack of preparation, many faculty and candidates within teacher preparation programs felt overwhelmed and stressed by the new assessment. Candidates did not know what to expect, nor did they know how to complete the tasks to meet the scoring criteria. This led to many candidates not passing this assessment. This also jeopardized the standing of some teacher preparation programs.

The EPP leaders of Crowne University had positioned themselves to provide their candidates with the support they needed to succeed on this assessment. A newly appointed faculty member, Xavier Ponton, had been trained as a scorer by the company that developed this assessment. He believed that he had the expertise to provide faculty with information and training so that they could assist candidates as they worked to understand the demands of the assessment. He also wanted to encourage more faculty members to be formally trained as scorers so they could consider revising the curriculum to address the gaps.

To support candidates in their quest to pass the assessment, Ponton developed a seven-part workshop, and over time he showed that the candidates he worked with were more likely to pass the assessment. The faculty were also directed to attend workshops that would help them better understand the requirements of the assessment and learn where candidates were having difficulty. However, as a junior faculty member, he found that veteran faculty were resistant to participating in the workshops he was leading. This left Ponton bewildered. He could not fathom why his colleagues acted in this way. Regardless of the support his efforts received from the EPP leaders, getting veteran faculty onboard was proving difficult. Candidates also were not enthusiastic about putting extra time into non-credit bearing workshops.

The Conflict/Challenge

When the teacher performance assessment results came in, Ponton was not surprised, though he was nervous about communicating the results to test takers, his chairperson, and the dean. He wondered about how successful he was as the lead trainer for the effort. He was concerned with whether the leaders would continue to support his efforts. Ponton did a self-assessment of his efforts and identified several things he, a junior faculty member, could have done differently to prepare the veteran faculty in a short span of time. These areas for improvement of the process included:

- **Communication:** Did he and program leaders adequately communicate the importance of the teacher performance assessment training to faculty? Did they explain the benefits of the teacher performance assessment for both faculty and candidates? Did they provide faculty with sufficient opportunities to ask questions and express their concerns?
- **Collaboration:** Did Ponton's enthusiasm involve the veteran faculty in the planning and implementation of the training? Did his efforts create a sense of community and support among faculty?

- **Differentiation:** Did he and the program leaders provide a mandate while offering a variety of training options, such as in-person workshops, online resources, and one-on-one support, and flexibility in how candidates would complete the training?

Questions for Discussion

1. When faced with external mandates, what steps should be taken by EPP leadership to ensure effective implementation and compliance?
2. What was the biggest challenge, or pilot error, for the newly appointed faculty member at the University in preparing for unpacking the teacher performance assessment?
3. How could the program leaders have created a supportive and collaborative environment for preparation for the assessment and not put all the pressure on the newly appointed faculty member?
4. What additional support should leadership have provided for this junior faculty member?
5. Given Ponton's positive analysis of the pilot, what should the next steps be?

TWENTY-TWO

A Question of Priorities

Nilda Soto Ruiz

AREAS FOR REFLECTION

- Implementing change
- Ethical/moral issues
- Leadership style

The Context

The Educational Leadership Program of a mid-sized university in a large city has over 400 students and continues to grow. The dean of the school is displeased with the administration of the program due to constant complaints from students, staff, faculty, the president of the University, and the State Education Department. He decided to find a new program chair and formed a search committee to recommend a candidate who could maintain enrollment growth, address organizational issues, and work with faculty and staff to improve the program's reputation. The committee selected Dr. Marzan, an educational leader with vast experience in various leadership positions in public education at both the K-12 and university levels, as the new chair of the program. Dr. Marzan will report directly to the dean and has indicated that he will present a comprehensive program improvement plan as soon as possible.

The program chair role is one that involves being a change agent, the critical link in leadership that can lead to significant and almost immediate positive changes in higher educational institutions (Chu, 2012). Dr. Marzan is charged by the dean to be this positive change agent and begins learning about the program and the larger school by interviewing faculty and staff to determine operating procedures and programs of study. The program is housed in a large office that Dr. Marzan will share with the program's assistant director and an administrative assistant. Although not orderly, the space facilitates communication among them.

The assistant director informs Dr. Marzan that she, as assistant director, is responsible for scheduling classes, assigning professors, hiring, and executing payroll contracts. She assures Dr. Marzan that he does not need to concern himself with any of those issues and that the administrative assistant reports directly to her. The assistant director also teaches two classes and supervises students enrolled in required internships.

Dr. Marzan requests to see the program of study and the proposal that was submitted to the State Education Department to certify the program. They are not readily available, so the assistant director must secure them from the Office of the Dean. Compounding the steepness of the learning curve, Dr. Marzan is bombarded with student complaints regarding the unavailability of some courses, the failure of some professors to inform students that a class has been cancelled, as well as grade challenges. Furthermore, students who have completed program requirements are not being recommended in a timely manner for state certification, thus preventing them from career advancement.

After interviews with the registrar, bursar, and Budget Office, Dr. Marzan informs the dean that he has decided to directly assume the responsibilities of scheduling, hiring, and budget allocations. He expects that the assistant director will complain, but the need to reorganize the office is imperative for efficiency and for the benefit of the students. He must count on the dean's total support.

Dr. Marzan conducts a thorough analysis of program scheduling and payroll. He discovers that there are no checks and balances and that the assistant director has been paid for classes that did not exist. Furthermore, the interns she assigned herself were never visited. In addition, she had a close family member teaching classes and supervising interns. Values, morals, and ethics are the very stuff of leadership and administrative life (Hodgkinson, 1991). Clearly, there was a lack of adherence to these principles by the assistant director.

The Conflict/Challenge

Dr. Marzan recommends the termination of the assistant director based on the evidence he has gathered. If the program is to improve and be held to high standards of performance and integrity, all staff must be held accountable for their actions. The assistant director could not be trusted. The dean needed to support the actions of the new department chair to correct the situation. The chair, in turn, must establish policies to ensure that procedures are followed to avoid misappropriation of funds and other improprieties.

Questions for Discussion

1. The dean, as an educational leader, was responsible for supporting the chair before replacement. What steps should a leader and supervisor take before determining that a change is justified?
2. Identify some of the steps that Dr. Marzan took to learn about the organization. What other actions can a leader take when assuming a new role?
3. How and when should Dr. Marzan communicate his priorities to the faculty and staff? What should he do to get support?
4. How would you describe Dr. Marzan's leadership style?
5. What guidance would you provide Dr. Marzan in working with senior administration, faculty, and staff to improve the department?

Reference

Chu, D. (2012). *The department chair primer* (2nd ed.). Jossey-Bass.
Hodgkinson, C. (1991). *Educational Leadership: The Moral Art.* SUNY Press.

PART IV

IMPLEMENTING AND ADAPTING TO CHANGE

TWENTY-THREE

Collaborator or Dictator?

Alan Sebel

AREAS FOR REFLECTION

- Leadership behaviors
- Collaboration
- Effectuating change
- Use of committees

The Context

PREMIER UNIVERSITY HAS JUST COMPLETED the search for a new dean for a large school within its organization and hired James Sylvester for the position. Dr. Sylvester has previous experience as a dean at a university in a neighboring state. The school he led was considerably smaller than the school at Premier. The school he is now heading has over 2,500 students, 50 full-time faculty, and 45 adjunct faculty members. The school has eight programs, each headed by a chairperson. None of the chairs applied for the position of dean. There is a significant number of support staff who serve as administrators, advisors to students, and more. During his interviews with the University Hiring Committee and in presentations to the faculty and staff, he presented himself as a collaborative and visionary leader with aspirations to be transformational in how he leads the school into the future. When questioned about this, he replied by referring to the work of Carl Lindberg (2022), that "Both transformational and visionary leadership are great for uniting people toward a shared long-term vision. Both styles build loyalty and trust in the leader through an emphasis on communication, transparency, and the use of Emotional Intelligence" (p. 14).

Dr. Sylvester stated repeatedly that he wholly welcomed faculty involvement in all decisions related to the several programs in the school. He indicated that all decisions, "as much as feasible," would be made by consensus with the various chairpersons and their faculty. Given this collaborative approach toward leading the school, the faculty and the University leaders overwhelmingly supported his candidacy.

Upon his arrival, the school was between accreditation cycles. In his early assessment of the organization, he determined that there was too little sharing between programs. He felt that this would impede progress as the school addressed the few areas of improvement identified during the last accreditation review. At his first faculty retreat, he stated, "I have conducted a thorough review of the conditions within the school, and one of the first things I want to address is breaking down the silos that have existed between the programs here." He had not discussed this with the chairpersons, nor did he include any of them or any other faculty members as he conducted and presented his assessment.

While the chairs understood the need for greater sharing and inter-program coordination, they felt that it should not have been presented to the faculty without prior discussion with them. After the retreat, several of the chairs openly objected to him having this kind of "openness" with faculty in a public forum, as they felt it was presenting them in a negative way with their faculty. They believed that he was blaming them for the development of the "silos," without examining the causes collaboratively with them. They earnestly believed that this undermined them with the faculty they led.

Over the next several months the dean established several committees. There was a Chairs Council, a Quality Assurance Committee, a Strategic Plan Committee, and a Data Review Committee, among others. The committees were established, ostensibly, to serve as a check-and-balance as the programs go through review. They would also help to break down the barriers to sharing ideas and, it was hoped, progress would be made toward addressing the criticisms that were identified in the previous accreditation. On paper and in discussion, this made perfect sense, and the dean's efforts were greeted enthusiastically and with great expectations.

The Conflict/Challenge

While presenting himself as a collaborative leader, the dean's initial conflict with the chairs revolved around how he introduced the need to break down "silos" at the faculty retreat. Then, even after he heard from several of the chairs about how introducing this at the retreat undermined them with their faculty, he further angered the chairs by identifying faculty members to be on the newly formed committees without input from the chairs. This further strained the relationship he had with some of the chairs.

As the committee process unfolded, members of the committee were presented with ideas and asked to provide feedback. They quickly learned that the input was only to "rubber stamp" decisions the dean had already made. Several faculty members made suggestions for how the school should address certain issues. Uniformly, these suggestions were listened to, and the dean would give an alternative and turn down the ideas presented by faculty. On several occasions the ideas would reappear a few weeks or months later as if they were the original ideas of the dean. This was immediately obvious to the committee members who heard their colleagues make the original proposals.

After several months, one of the faculty members openly challenged the dean about this at a committee meeting. The faculty member was joined in her protest by other members of one committee. As a group they all resigned from the committee. They stated that they had agreed to be on the committee as they saw it as an opportunity to work with the dean, collaboratively, to identify problematic areas within the school that needed to be changed to strengthen the programs, break down barriers to sharing of effective practices across programs, and address continuous improvement. They soon realized that the only function of the committees was to say "yes" to whatever the dean had already determined needed to be done. They felt that their expertise, historical perspective, and knowledge of the school were not valued by the dean. This group decided to write this complaint in a formal letter of protest and send it to the entire faculty. After doing so, it made its way to the attention of the provost. The provost decided to actively investigate the complaint.

Questions for Discussion

1. What mistakes did Dr. Sylvester make when he first started in his position as dean?
2. How could Dr. Sylvester have avoided the issues that developed between him and the chairpersons?
3. If you were Dr. Sylvester, what would you do on your first 100 days on the job?

4. Change is difficult. What might Dr. Sylvester have done differently if he wanted to change the existing conditions he found after his assessment of the school's programs?

Reference

Lindberg, C. (2022, August 20). *Transformational vs. visionary leadership—CEO Reflections #16*. Leadership ahoy. https://www.leadershipahoy.com/transformational-vs-visionary-leadership/#:~:text=What%20are%20the%20differences%20between,overlooking%20short%2Dterm%20operational%20concerns

TWENTY-FOUR

College Life Beyond the Crisis

Shoshanah Findling

AREAS FOR REFLECTION

- Crisis management
- Delivery of instruction
- Enrollment management

The Context

GREENFIELD IS A MID-SIZED PRIVATE university with a student population of 15,000 located in the New York metropolitan area. The University has both undergraduate and graduate professional schools located in various boroughs and towns. The student population across the various schools is diverse in many ways related to age, race, religion, ethnicity, and language. The student body is composed of many non-traditional students who work full-time, have families to raise, or are returning to school after making a career change. A small percentage of the student body enters directly from high school. The University draws most of its students from within the state and relies on tuition and donations for its operating budget.

During the COVID-19 pandemic, the University rapidly transitioned from in-person instruction to a video conference modality, while simultaneously increasing an already strong online asynchronous footprint. Professional development was offered to faculty to prepare them for remote learning and the assessment of student performance. The federal government provided some assistance to businesses and post-secondary institutions; however, the federal aid stopped when the significant impact of the pandemic diminished.

Since the recent recession of 2007-2008, birthrates have declined significantly. This resulted in a decline in enrollment in most colleges and universities across the country. In addition, since the pandemic, nearly 500,000 people have moved from the New York metropolitan area to other regions in the country due to rising housing costs, quality of life issues, and an increase in crime (Raisinghani, 2023). Many businesses continued to allow their employees to work from home after the national emergency ended. Employers discovered that many tasks and meetings could be completed remotely.

As COVID-19 restrictions eased, and Greenfield considered reopening, a vaccine mandate was implemented for all employees and students. A limited number of approved medical or religious exemptions were offered. Some of the schools and programs reopened, allowing for in-person classes. One example was the Nursing Program in the School of Health Sciences. Other schools and programs at Greenfield saw an increased request by students for online or virtual instruction, and a decreased desire to return to in-person classes. Greenfield met this demand, and as a result enrollment remained stable.

The Conflict/Challenge

As planning regarding delivery of instruction was ongoing, some faculty and students continued to voice their preferences. Some employees and students preferred to work and study remotely while others wanted to resume in-person operations. The group that wanted to work on-site felt they were outnumbered by those wanting to work remotely. This latter group was more vocal about its position. Among those favoring in-person teaching and learning, some felt that video conference instruction was insufficient for social-emotional reasons. They had already seen evidence of inadequate delivery of remote instruction, where some students failed to remain engaged. Further, many employees and students faced challenges accessing reliable online connections. Students in favor of in-person classes also felt that their learning style was best supported by a traditional classroom setting. Morale and productivity among staff and instructors declined. Some shared that they feared losing their jobs if one side prevailed over the other. Others feared returning to campus for health-related and other reasons, while also noting the reported increase in crime on the mass transit system.

Consider yourself at Greenfield. As the head of your school or program, you are responsible for making the schedule for the new semester, assigning the instructors, and overseeing advisement for 500 students. In a typical year, around 100 course sections are needed. You will have to decide whether to schedule in-person classes. With a significant number of individuals representing both sides of the in-person vs. remote debate, how would you proceed?

Questions for Discussion

1. As the program head, what must you consider before making decisions about this issue?
2. What constituencies are affected by the decisions you make? What might their concerns be?
3. What are the potential risks for the institution resulting from your decisions?
4. How might the handling of this situation contribute to or detract from a sense of community and teamwork within the institution?
5. Where should education take place: virtually/remotely, live and in-person, or in a hybrid format? Should this change be based on the academic level of the students (undergraduate, graduate, professional studies) and the field of study (medical, education, business, technology)?
6. As a higher education administrator, how much input should various stakeholders have in the operational decisions that you make?
7. How much influence does your own value system have on the administrative decisions you need to make?

Reference

Raisinghani, V. (2023, November 16). *New York City has lost 5.3% of its population*. Moneywise. https://finance.yahoo.com/news/york-city-lost-5-3-100000482.html

TWENTY-FIVE

Creating a Virtual Community of Practice

Gitta Jaroslawicz-Neufeld

AREAS FOR REFLECTION

- Student engagement
- Communities of practice
- Remote learning
- Introducing emerging technologies

The Context

Touro University's Graduate School of Education (GSE) recently welcomed the first cohort of a new graduate program, the master's degree in Jewish Childhood Education/Special Education. The program was designed for educators who work with general education and with children with special needs attending religious day schools and yeshivas. All the degree candidates were already employed as teachers in these private schools. Because the program attracted teachers from the tri-state area, a hybrid instructional model was developed. Teacher candidates had the option to attend in-person classes once a week, in either Brooklyn or Manhattan. For the second class, they could attend virtually. In other words, candidates who chose Brooklyn as their site would attend class there on Mondays, and then attend the Wednesday class in Manhattan virtually. Candidates who opted for Manhattan would access the Brooklyn site class virtually on Mondays, and then attend in-person on Wednesdays in Manhattan. While we recognized that this was not ideal for developing relationships, both among members of the cohort and with the instructors, the decision was made to implement this model in the hope of attracting more candidates from a wider variety of locations, thus adding to the diversity of the student body and expanding the nascent program's visibility in the Jewish Education sphere. With only 12 students in the initial cohort, the model appeared workable.

When COVID-19 struck, all schools were closed to in-person instruction. Our candidates were already experiencing remote instruction for part of their program, which allowed us to pivot quickly, and in fact to serve as a resource to other programs and schools in implementing virtual instruction. We also realized this model would significantly impact the cohesiveness of the group of candidates. They would no longer have the opportunity to interact or socialize with at least half of their peers on a regular basis. Added to this was the stress of changes to instruction that they themselves were experiencing as teachers due to the pandemic, as well as the novelty of the modality and its unique constraints, the inequity of access to resources that some of their students faced, and the fear of COVID-19 itself.

Our instructors would begin each session with a "check-in" on how the candidates were managing, and heard the candidates consistently say that they were "feeling lonely in [their] own home[s]." Candidates missed their colleagues and the unscheduled ad-lib interactions they normally engaged in on a day-to-day basis. While they were busy with, and often overwhelmed by, engagement in a new model of teaching and learning, they expressed the need for consistent collegial input and mutual encouragement. This was particularly evident with the newer teachers, who had less professional background and experience and relied heavily on their colleagues and supervisors for advice and assistance.

The Conflict/Challenge

We recognized the need to create a venue for professional interaction and moral support. Although we allowed time in each of our sessions, as noted above, for candidates to express their concerns and seek solutions, that time was limited. Additionally, we wished to model the creation of a Community of Practice (COP). In a COP, participants join to share knowledge, experience, and insights as a means of problem-solving, promotion of best practices, professional development, and mutual support (Wenger & Snyder, 2000). Involvement in a COP enhances group members' shared identity as stakeholders in the COP's focus (Wenger et al., 2002)—in this case, as educators. At the same time, we realized that there were increased demands on our candidates' time as they dealt with the educational and emotional needs of their students and the students' families.

Our solution was to create a JESN (the course code for course offerings within our program) WhatsApp group. The ability to communicate "on demand" with peers was an attractive feature, as was the ability to share documents, links, and media. The informal nature of WhatsApp communication provided a layer of comfort. We consciously made the choice not to include any program personnel in the group, instead asking for candidates to volunteer to serve as chat administrators. We left it to the group to decide on group norms and expectations. We informed all instructors of the group's existence and encouraged them to refer to it as appropriate.

As the pandemic waned, we considered returning to our previous model of instruction. We found, as did many other programs at the Graduate School of Education, that our candidates preferred the virtual environment. We assumed that given the heightened level of comfort and expertise that the candidates now had with a virtual classroom environment, there would no longer be the need for the WhatsApp group. We casually suggested that it end. We were surprised to find that our candidates not only wanted the group to continue, but they also wanted to remain in the group even after graduation. As one candidate who did not generally engage in social media said, "It's like having the teachers' room in my pocket!" While we are not privy to the chat contents, our students report robust and meaningful interactions on a regular basis.

Questions for Discussion

1. What tools, in addition to WhatsApp, could have been used to create a Community of Practice?
2. What is the optimum balance between instructor/program input and candidate agency and independence?
3. How can we address the diverse levels of comfort with technology, especially considering certain candidates' cultural and religious sensitivities?
4. Given that instructors and students in higher education are comfortable with virtual instruction, how important is it that education return to in-class instruction?
5. What is the responsibility of higher education to adopt new technologies, such as video conferencing, simulations, virtual and augmented reality, AI (Artificial Intelligence), etc.?

References

Wenger, E. C., McDermott, R., & Snyder, W. M. (2002). *Cultivating communities of practice.* Harvard Business Press.

Wenger, E. C., & Snyder, W. M. (2000). Communities of Practice: The organizational frontier. *Harvard Business Review, 78*(1), 139–145.

TWENTY-SIX

Leading from the Middle: Perspective of a Newly Hired Leader

Olga DeJesus-Diaz

AREAS FOR REFLECTION

- Individual leadership and the institution's culture
- Life as a middle leader
- Academic integrity
- Adapting to a new culture

The Context

The Dean of the School of Social and Behavioral Sciences at a small, private, traditional liberal arts college in a suburban area of New York has recently hired Dr. Young as the new department chair to lead one of four departments in the school: the Teacher Education Department. Research indicates that most chairs receive little or no training to prepare them for the demands of their new roles. They may not understand the tasks they will need to perform, how much time they will have to spend on parts of the job, and what the emotional and social requirements are (Chu, 2012). Although Dr. Young is new to this institution, he is not new to the field and has many years of prior experience in educational leadership in higher education. The Teacher Education Department offers both undergraduate and graduate programs and is comprised of one administrative assistant, eight full-time faculty, and a large pool of part-time faculty.

As an experienced leader, Dr. Young understands that the first order of business is to take some time to acclimate to the institution's culture and develop a rapport with all constituents: students, faculty, and the institution's community at large. However, Dr. Young has quickly learned that this will not be an easy task in an institution where the personnel have been there for many years and with an established culture of "this is our way, and this is how it has always been done."

Registration for the spring semester had just opened when Mary, a student from the Secondary Education graduate program came to meet with Dr. Young, the department chair who is also the student's academic advisor. Together they review the recommended program pathway to plan what would be the final spring semester of courses required for degree completion. During the advising session, both Mary and Dr. Young noticed a conflict in Mary's schedule, as the last two courses she needed to graduate were offered at the same time. Considering that Dr. Young was very familiar with degree requirements and state requirements, he did not hesitate to find an approved alternative course from one of the other programs in the Teacher Education Department that would work in the student's schedule as a course substitution. The student left Dr. Young's office very pleased with the resolution and excited to start the spring semester.

The Conflict/Challenge

As advised, Mary enrolled in two courses, both taught by Assistant Professor Smith, a junior faculty member in the department. At the beginning of the first week of the spring semester, Dr. Smith requested a meeting with Dr. Young. During the meeting, Dr. Smith questioned Dr. Young's rationale for recommending that Mary register for a course outside of her program. Dr. Young proceeded to explain to Dr. Smith that although the recommended course for substitution was outside of her major, it was still a course within the department, close in content to the one required for her program of study, and that completion of this course allowed Mary to: (1) complete the required number of credits for her degree, and (2) satisfy the state's requirement of the preparation program.

Despite the explanation provided by the department chair, Dr. Smith continued to insist that an alternative course be recommended as a substitute. She felt that the course recommended by the chair was not the best fit for Mary. Confused as to why Dr. Smith was insisting that Mary drop one of her two courses and register for another, Dr. Young finally asked the question, "Why do you feel so strongly that Mary drop one of your two courses?"

Dr. Smith's response revealed the true root cause of the conflict. She proceeded to explain that although the two courses had different codes and titles, the content was the same, and Mary would be bored by taking two courses that had the same content. The more Dr. Smith explained, the more bewildered the department chair became as he was learning that this faculty member was teaching two different courses with the same content and assignments. Not only did the new chair realize that the sequencing of this program created a scheduling issue, but also that the curriculum was repetitive across programs, and, in some cases, faculty may not have been taking the initiative to differentiate content between parallel courses.

Dr. Young concluded the meeting with Dr. Smith by standing by his decision that it was in the best interest of Mary to remain in the two courses and strongly suggested that Dr. Smith modify the curriculum and assignments in the alternative course to meet the needs of the students in the other program. Unsatisfied with the department chair's decision and recommendation, Dr. Smith left the office and proceeded to email Mary.

Dr. Smith wrote that the alternative course was not a good fit for her degree completion. She tried to influence Mary to complain to Dr. Young regarding dropping the course and finding a different alternative. This confused Mary.

Given that this situation had escalated, Dr. Young knew that something had to be done to implement immediate change to prevent this from happing in future terms. Dr. Young identified that courses in different programs listed as alternatives were, in fact, the exact same courses with different course codes. He proceeded to consult with the dean with the hope that they could plan and implement actions for improvement.

It was a failed effort! When Dr. Young met with Dr. Seltzer, the school's dean, to inform her of the issue, Dr. Seltzer informed Dr. Young that she was aware of the issue of the "double dip" of the curriculum between the two education programs and that this issue came up often when students from one program would want to enroll in the other or when advisors would recommend a course substitution. The dean recommended that Dr. Young reverse his decision of recommending that the student remain in the course and that the faculty member modify the curriculum. The dean also advised the chair to find another course outside of the department to be used as an elective for degree credit completion.

Dr. Young was amazed at the dean's reaction to the matter; however, he proceeded to comply with the request. He understood that he was now leading from the middle in an institution with a culture to which he was unaccustomed. He realized that if he wanted to effectuate change, he would have to figure out how to influence the many stakeholders.

Questions for Discussion

1. How would you describe the issues and actions that led to this conflict?
2. Do you consider the actions of each of the main players, Dr. Smith, Dr. Young, and Dr. Seltzer, to be ethical and professional? Why or why not?
3. How would you compare the leadership styles of Dr. Young and Dr. Seltzer?
4. As the school dean or senior manager, what recommendation would you have given Dr. Young as she sought out support with this situation?

Reference

Chu, D. (2012). *The department chair primer* (2nd ed.). Jossey-Bass.

TWENTY-SEVEN

When Admissions Protocols Become Murky: Unintended Consequences

Sarah J. Klugman

AREAS FOR REFLECTION

- Admissions processes
- Managing resources
- Equity and access

The Context

THE COVID-19 PANDEMIC LED TO new challenges for undergraduate admissions committees in many universities and colleges. One problem that persists is whether to reinstate the requirement that students take the SAT or the ACT for admissions. Because many prestigious universities have become SAT- and ACT-optional, many smaller universities and colleges feel that to stay competitive, they too need to remain test-optional. If the SAT and ACT are no longer required, new admissions metrics may need to be determined. Some colleges are grappling with alternative admissions requirements that can be applied holistically, without bias, to all prospective applicants. For Harvard (2024), as an example, this is what students see when they query about whether the school is test-optional:

> Students who do not submit standardized test scores will not be disadvantaged in their application process. Applicants will be considered on the basis of what they have presented, and students are encouraged to send whatever materials they believe would convey their accomplishments in secondary school and their promise for the future.

Alternatively, a number of colleges and universities are asking students for a portfolio of curated and graded work that shows their growth and abilities, while others are requiring students to take a placement exam developed by the institution and scored by the department chair. In addition, a personal interview with an admissions counselor is required.

The Conflict/Challenge

When colleges decided not to require either the ACT or SAT as a criterion for admissions, many institutions developed their own procedures. In some instances, this was a two-tiered process: The steps involved both the application and admissions processes. Applicants are required to submit a portfolio and/or other material to demonstrate college readiness. After an initial review of the application, the applicant would then take a college-developed placement examination and participate in an interview. These added processes require additional time and personnel, and any delay may cause some applicants to withdraw from consideration.

Questions for Discussion

1. What do you see as the best possible scenario for an admissions process for a school that is test-optional?
2. How do you manage this application and admissions process?
3. What are other possible metrics for consideration for admission?
4. What pitfalls do you see with this process for admission?
5. Considering the admissions process at your own institution, what can be done to reduce the potential that implicit bias might impact the decision process?

Reference

Harvard University. (2024). *Admissions update for the 2023-2026 application cycles.* https://college.harvard.edu/about/news-announcements/admission-application-considerations-class-2026

PART V

INTRODUCING NEW TECHNOLOGIES

TWENTY-EIGHT

Faculty Discretion vs. Departmental Oversight

Yair Maman

AREAS FOR REFLECTION

- Peer supervision
- Faculty discretion
- Leadership style
- Faculty/chairpersons' relationships

The Context

THE MASTER OF SCIENCE IN School Counseling is a three-year program within Fledgling University's Graduate School of Education (GSE). During the second and third years, at the practicum and internship stages, respectively, degree candidates are engaged in peer supervision. The Wagner and Smith (1979) model, enhanced by the work of Mowbray (1987) and Starling and Baker (2000), is geared toward guiding peer supervision. Candidates form groups and consider peer supervision as a process in which counselors-in-training help one another become more effective and skillful by using their relationships and professional skills with one another (Mowbray, 1987; Seligman, 1978; Starling & Baker, 2000; Wagner & Smith, 1979). The clinical instructor is responsible for assigning candidates to groups. Within each group, the following roles are assigned by the course instructor:

- Manager or Facilitator—ensures that the group stays on task, is focused, and has room for everyone in the conversation.
- Recorder—keeps a record of those in the group and the roles they play in the group and records critical points from the discussion.
- Spokesperson or Presenter—presents the group's ideas to the rest of the class but relies on the Recorder's notes to guide the report.

- Reflector or Strategy Analyst—observes team dynamics and guides the consensus-building process, helping group members reach a common conclusion.

The instructor can set up the time, place, and format of group meetings (mornings, evenings, in-class, or synchronous video conferencing).

Professor Smith was assigned a Clinical Internship course in the program. He has been at the University for more than ten years. He has extensive clinical supervision experience. He works closely with the chairperson, who also has extensive clinical supervision experience. The chairperson embedded peer supervision in the Practicum course. The chairperson also teaches that course, which is a prerequisite to the Internship course. Professor Smith then instructs the same group of students for the Internship course.

Prior to teaching the Internship course for the first time, Professor Smith took and passed an intensive course focused on how to facilitate lectures through video conferencing techniques. The chairperson also gave him specific guidelines and instructions for implementing peer supervision in the Internship course.

During the first class session, Professor Smith relayed that the peer supervision part of the Internship course would be conducted in person on-site. This was not well-received by candidates. They argued that in the previous Clinical course (Practicum), peer supervision was conducted by video conferencing. They further argued that they feel more comfortable continuing with the same format. If he insisted on conducting the peer supervision on-site, they would complain to the chairperson about this change in the meeting format. When Professor Smith said that it was a better learning experience for them to meet face-to-face for peer supervision, the candidates petitioned the chairperson to intervene to keep the current video conferencing format for peer supervision.

The Conflict/Challenge

Following the candidates' complaints, the chairperson arranged a meeting with the candidates to discuss their perspectives about the change. Professor Smith sought the chairperson's support to change the peer-supervision format to in-class meetings. He protested the chairperson's decision to meet with candidates, stating that it would undermine efforts to convince candidates of the best option for peer supervision activities: in-class meetings. To support his argument for the meetings to be in person, Professor Smith relied on his experience at another institution, where he observed that candidates were more engaged with peer supervision when meetings were conducted in person.

The chairperson met with the candidates at the arranged time and asked them to freely express why they felt that it was essential to keep the video conferencing format. In their confidential conversation, several candidates indicated that they felt that meeting remotely was productive and liked to continue their positive experiences from the practicum. They elucidated that it was the best way for discussing culturally relevant cases in peer supervision. They felt that they were able to cross-community lines by *slowly* warming up to their fellow classmates. They thought that they could only progress to deeper discussions with deeper meaning from the comfort and safety of video conferencing. Moreover, the candidates said that commuting to meet in person takes away from much needed time for addressing mental health issues with the children they serve in their communities.

One of the main goals of the Counselor Education program was to promote inter-community collaboration. Another goal was to promote safety in expressing sensitive ideas. The chairperson immediately saw that there was a measured advantage for continuing with the remote format, as it promoted bridging the cultural divide and assisted in crossing community lines. The chairperson also noted the group's contention that emotional safety is an important factor that contributes to perceived benefits for the group and a feeling of safety. It also helps in establishing a supportive community where everyone is invited to open up in a safe space (Cirucci, 2023; Haas et al., 2020). As such, the chairperson was cognizant of the benefits of videoconferencing as it helped the candidates "open up." As far as being culturally relevant, the chairperson kept in mind that it was, indeed, a main overarching goal of the program to work towards achieving cross-cultural understanding. Intercultural communication has a way of supporting positive impact on decision-making. Effective technologies for intercultural communication can include e-mail, teleconferencing combined with e-meetings, and other ways to support team rooms and cultural diversity locally and worldwide (Canto et al., 2013).

After meeting with the students, the chairperson decided that he needed to explain the context of how the Guidance program was developed to Professor Smith. He wanted the professor to understand that the program is heavily dependent upon the chairperson's direct involvement with recruiting the students from communities reflective of the metropolitan area served by the University. The chairperson further detailed the philosophy of the program's design. He indicated that while candidates are trained for self-care and for seeing a smaller perspective in the introductory course, in the Practicum and the Internship, they are working on a bigger scale to leverage resources on a community level to meet the needs of those they counsel. He stated that divisive issues, such as the stigma of mental healthcare, evaporate faster when we focus on what unites us: similar mental health issues across community lines.

The chairperson focused on addressing two areas of the candidates' concerns and concluded that, at the time, the most effective way for peer supervision was through video conferencing, as it allowed for both the comfort of not traveling and provided a safe space for addressing the cultural divide. The chairperson reflected that while it may be beneficial to expand to in-person meetings (preferably at local sites in diverse communities), for the time being, it would be counterproductive to change the format as it may irreparably change positive group dynamics.

Questions for Discussion

1. Under what circumstances might Professor Smith have the right to change the format for peer supervision?
2. Was the chairperson correct in meeting with the candidates without the professor present? If so, why? If not, why not? What would you have done differently?
3. How does the concept of academic freedom play a part in this case?
4. To what extent should such decisions be made by the chairperson or by the instructor?
5. How could this dispute best be resolved?
6. At what point should faculty reach out to get chairperson support for controversial decisions?

References

Canto, S., Jauregi, K., & van den Bergh, H. (2013). Integrating cross-cultural interaction through video-communication and virtual worlds in foreign language teaching programs: Is there an added value? *ReCALL, 25*(1), 105–121.

Cirucci, A. M. (2023). Zoom affordances and identity: A case study. *Social media + Society, 9*(1), 20.

Haas, S., De Soete, A., & Ulstein, G. (2020). Zooming through Covid: Fostering safe communities of critical reflection via online writers' group interaction. *Double Helix, 8*, 1–10

Mowbray, C. (1987). A proposed model for peer supervision. *Counselor Education and Supervision, 27*, 53–60.

Seligman, L. (1978). The relationship of facilitative functioning to effective peer supervision. *Counselor Education and Supervision, 17*, 254–260.

Starling, P. V., & Baker, S. B. (2000). Structured peer group practicum supervision: Supervisees' perceptions of supervision theory. *Counselor Education & Supervision, 39*(3), 162–176.

Wagner, C. A., & Smith, J. P. (1979). Peer supervision: Toward more effective training. *Counselor Education and Supervision, 18*, 288–293.

TWENTY-NINE

Open Educational Resources (OER): Is It Worth It?

Sara Tabaei

AREAS FOR REFLECTION

- Adopting new technology
- Free or low-cost OER textbooks vs. latest edition tradeoff
- Advocating for reduced costs

The Context

OPEN METRO IS METRO UNIVERSITY'S Open Education Resources (OER) initiative. With this project, Metro Libraries aim to reduce the cost of textbooks for students, increase student retention and success, raise awareness of OER, and assist faculty in selecting, adopting, adapting, and creating open textbooks for their courses.

Within two years of its decision to pursue OER, Metro Libraries was awarded a National Institutes of Health (NIH) grant which, though modest, played an essential role in advancing the initiative in a few ways.

First, it captured the attention of senior management. The grant's award affirmed the value and potential of the OER initiative, as evidenced by the recognition and support from an external funding agency.

Second, the establishment of an OER faculty fellowship, accompanied by a small stipend, was made possible by the grant's funding. The idea of a faculty fellowship, created by the library, was novel. Deans and chairs encouraged their faculty to apply for the fellowship, as they saw it as a professional development opportunity. As a result, five faculty members were awarded $500 each. The success of the first round of fellowships did not go unnoticed. When the provost was approached for partnership with the OER initiative, her office agreed to fund the next round of fellowships. The Office of the Provost allocated funds for three faculty fellowship programs but indicated that funding would likely not be available in the future.

Another benefit was the financial impact by way of a return on investment. Within four years and two cohorts of faculty fellows, Open Metro saved over half-a-million dollars. Almost 50% of the savings was due to the two fellowship cohorts. In other words, just a small financial contribution from Metro yielded a huge amount of financial savings for students. Using the first fellowship cohort as an example, with an investment of $500 per faculty fellow, or $2,500 total, five fellows have gone on to produce over $200,000 in savings for their students since the initiation of the program.

The Conflict/Challenge

Unfortunately, by year three, no funding is available. By not receiving further funding, the library will lose the faculty fellowship program which has had a great financial impact on students and the school to date. From the beginning, the Open Metro program was well-received by various undergraduate departments, including the Psychology, Biology, Mathematics, Economics, and Business Departments. Many faculty members were looking for alternatives to traditional textbooks because their students could not afford to buy them, and this provided an alternative.

Based on a study with the Metro Undergraduate Psychology Department, the library discovered that instead of spending the money on a pricey textbook, students typically used the money saved for food, rent, babysitters, and more.

Aside from the financial benefits of OER, using OER in classes has been repeatedly proven to positively influence academic outcomes. Various studies indicate that students perform as well or better in classes that utilize OER versus classes with traditional textbooks (Magro & Tabaei, 2020; Parsons, 2023; Wynants & Dennis, 2023). Moreover, more educational institutions, such as Tidewater Community College (2021) and Cosumnes River College (2024), not only have designated low-cost or zero-cost course sections but also have introduced Zero Textbook Cost (ZTC) degrees. This highlights the rising significance of implementing OER in the academic setting.

Implementing an OER program is a critical service for students and faculty. It also adds significant value for accreditation purposes, as the OER initiative is firmly aligned with the school's mission, particularly in its commitment to serving underserved student populations.

Questions for Discussion

1. What could have been another approach to starting this initiative?
2. What steps should Open Metro take to continue to generate funding for the successful OER fellowship program?
3. How could you build support from other constituencies to continue the fellowship program?
4. Other than funding, what other incentives could be used to encourage more development and usage of OER?
5. How can the rising college tuition costs influence the perceived value of the OER initiative and its alignment with broader concerns?

References

Consumnes River College. (2024). *Zero textbook costs at Consumnes River College.* https://crc.losrios.edu/admissions/enroll-in-classes/zero-textbook-cost-degrees-and-certificates/zero-textbook-costs

Magro, J., & Tabaei, S. V. (2020). Results from a Psychology OER pilot program: Faculty and student perceptions, cost savings, and academic outcomes. *Open Praxis, 12*(1), 83–99. https://doi.org/10.5944/openpraxis.12.1.1007

Parsons, J. W. (2023). *OER and no-cost textbook-based courses and their impact on student performance at a rural community college* (Publication No. 2859423179) [Doctoral dissertation, Wingate University]. ProQuest One Academic.

Tidewater Community College. (2021). *TCC expands role in zero-textbook-cost education.* https://www.tcc.edu/program-highlights/tcc-expands-role-in-zero-textbook-cost-education/

Wynants, S., & Dennis, J. (2023). Redesigning a research methods course with personalized, interactive OER: A case study of student perceptions and performance. *Journal of Scholarship and Teaching and Learning, 22*(1), 138–153.

THIRTY

Transforming Teacher Training: Dr. Smith's Journey Implementing an AI-Based Teaching Simulation Platform

Jasmin Cowin

AREAS FOR REFLECTION

- Administrative skepticism
- Funding hurdles
- Overcoming student resistance
- Implementing new technologies

The Context

Over a span of four years, Dr. Iris Smith, an associate professor at Anywhere University's Graduate School of Education, embarked on a journey to integrate an AI-powered simulation platform into the teacher training curriculum of one program in a graduate school. Dr. Smith saw an opportunity to reorient the goals of teacher education by emphasizing the development of ATL (Approaches to Learning) skills in the context of designing experiential learning through integrating this AI-powered teaching simulation platform. The narrative of this case study will go into the challenges she encountered, including administrative skepticism, funding obstacles, and significant student resistance, ultimately culminating in a student conflict.

The AI-powered simulation platform is an innovative online simulator designed to enhance teacher preparation. As a scalable platform using AI, it aims to improve pedagogical expertise by recreating typical classroom challenges that a teacher will address in today's diverse classrooms. These models are grounded in modern psychology, cognitive science, and neuroscience concepts, including the Five-Factor Model of psychology. The Five-Factor Model is a widely recognized and accepted personality theory among psychologists. It proposes that personality can be distilled into five fundamental factors, often represented by the acronym CANOE. These factors are Conscientiousness, Agreeableness, Neuroticism, Openness to Experience, and Extraversion. These Five Factors are notably stable throughout most of an individual's lifetime and have predictive validity concerning important life outcomes, such as an individual's education level and overall health. Since 2003, this platform has featured emotional intelligence avatars in diverse classroom settings, providing users with authentic experiences.

Dr. Smith's goals for implementation of this simulator into a foundational graduate course were to achieve targeted outcomes for teacher candidates, including:

- Increased confidence and technology self-efficacy in teaching;
- Enhanced knowledge of instructional strategies and classroom management techniques;
- Improved understanding of students' cognitive, emotional, and cultural differences;
- Increased retention in the teaching field post-graduation; and
- Robust data collection for faculty to monitor candidate progress for accreditation purposes.

Dr. Smith's ultimate plan was to introduce and use simulations to focus on high-leverage practices (HLP) to support teacher candidates' experiential learning. HLP are fundamental teaching strategies that effective teachers should be able to use consistently. In addition, she wanted her colleagues to see that AI-powered simulation environments allow for repeated practice and in-depth exploration of HLP post-simulator implementation. Teacher candidates would have the opportunity to interact with a virtual classroom and receive immediate feedback about their decisions. The faculty would also have access to this valuable practical data.

Dr. Smith applied for several university grants for funding to implement this on-demand practice simulation tool, which could potentially augment or replace some traditional field experiences. Its implementation would represent a significant shift in teacher training, leveraging AI-powered simulations to enhance the preparation and effectiveness of teacher candidates. In each instance, her application for a grant was denied without explanation.

This made it difficult to understand what needed to be changed for future applications.

Over the course of three years Dr. Smith tested out the simulator through alternative means by working with educators in the Middle East through a virtual program she offered at no cost. She published her findings in peer-reviewed journals and presented them at international conferences. She then returned to her administrators, including a new dean and a new chair. During her conversations with them, they raised concerns about the allocation of funds for simulation and AI-powered technology and its potential impact on the quality of teacher training. Despite these challenges, Dr. Smith remained committed to her vision, seeing the AI-powered simulator as a crucial tool for preparing future educators in an increasingly digital world. Meanwhile, AI expanded in usage and recognition, which Dr. Smith highlighted to persuade her new chair and new dean, who both became more open to her initiative. She demonstrated extensive evidence that simulated environments statistically correlate with real classrooms for developing teaching skills. Finally, Dr. Smith secured a private grant, supporting her belief in the simulator's potential for transformative teacher training, and the tool was incorporated into course XYZ for teacher candidates to complete virtual fieldwork. All other courses featured in-person fieldwork.

The Assignment:

Assignment Description—

- Virtual Fieldwork: Ten hours teaching in simModules
- Instructional Synopsis/Reflection

About the AI-powered simulator—

The AI-powered simulator is a web-based virtual classroom environment populated with simulated students. Simulated students have artificial emotional intelligence. They smile, cry, become frustrated, raise their hands, seek attention, and show signs of stress. They respond in very individual ways to tasks assigned, tone of voice used, and classroom management strategies employed.

Grounded in established theories of cognition, emotion, social behavior, and more, the simulator provides users authentic experiences and has been vetted through a decade of continuous research, field testing, and clinical practice. The characters are virtual, but the learning is very real. We will go through your training together.

Part of your deliverables will be teaching in the simulated environment and reflecting on your simulated classroom experience.

Points to include:

- Professional Development: Consider how the reflection connects to your professional growth. Reflect on the new knowledge or skills you have acquired and how you plan to apply them in future teaching endeavors. Identify any professional development opportunities or resources that could enhance your teaching practice.
- Conclusion: Summarize your main insights and key takeaways from the reflection. Consider how the experience has influenced your teaching philosophy or approach. Reflect on any changes or adjustments you plan to make to your future teaching practices based on your analysis.

Remember, a teacher's written reflection is a personal and subjective piece, so feel free to express your thoughts, emotions, and reflections openly. It is an opportunity for self-discovery, growth, and the enhancement of your teaching practice.

The Conflict/Challenge

Several weeks into the semester, discontent among students regarding the simulator exploded openly on a student forum. Students expressed frustration that the assignments felt arbitrary and detracted precious time and focus from genuine teaching experiences. Some students struggled with the new interface while others did not like the AI-generated feedback. In the meantime, several teacher candidates felt they should be exempt from using such technology and should instead be permitted to do their fieldwork in-person.

The conflict reached its peak four weeks into the semester when Dr. Smith encountered direct opposition from her students. A defining moment was an e-mail from a student, A.B., expressing skepticism about the value of the simulated experience: "*Hi Professor, Can I ask why our hours can't be done in person with actual students vs. in a computer-generated classroom? I do not see how this is more beneficial than the real-life experiences we encounter daily in reality. I would appreciate any clarification.*"

Dr. Smith checked the student's log-in times in the simulation platform and noticed the student had signed in but completed only one 20-minute teaching set without accessing the introductory help videos.

Dr. Smith's response was the following: *I hear your frustration and hope you have completed the survey about your experience with the simulations. Everyone who is in the simulation has a different experience, and I do want to hear about yours. How many hours have you been in the simulation so far? Yours, Dr. Smith*

After reflecting on several other similarly worded e-mails and discussion posts in her Learning Management System, she created a course announcement.

> Announcement: Addressing Concerns about Using Simulations in Virtual Fieldwork in Course XYZ
>
> Candidates,
>
> I have received feedback regarding the use of the simulator in our Course XYZ. I deeply value your perspectives and understand the apprehensions that come with interacting with and learning new technology.
>
> Our decision to integrate simulations into the curriculum is rooted in preparing you for the contemporary shifts in education. More and more school districts across the U.S. are turning towards AI-enhanced methodologies for teacher observations. For instance, an article titled "Can AI Do Teacher Observations and Deliver PD?" (2023) points out, "The Spokane school district in Washington state is trying out an artificial-intelligence-powered instructional coach to help teachers evaluate and strengthen their classroom practices" (para. 1). This evolution is not isolated; another report titled, "How Artificial Intelligence Could Help Teachers Do a Better Job," (2018) states that, "Thanks to advances in artificial intelligence, teams of education researchers and computer scientists are experimenting with how to build systems that can 'see' into and 'listen' in on classrooms and instantly analyze the quality of classroom instruction. Technology is improving rather rapidly now, thanks to improvements in natural language processing and automatic speech recognition. At the same time, it takes an enormous amount of work just to teach the robots how to observe one

micro aspect of a classroom at a time" (para. 2). In an experiment, researchers built an algorithmic teacher observer for analyzing the quality of instruction.

I cannot evaluate these new developments without deep concerns about our profession and our professional independence, but at the same time, there is a responsibility to prepare you, our candidates, for different systems and possibilities.

This emerging landscape demonstrates that as the field of education evolves, so must our preparation methods. However, I want to clarify that our aim is not to replace the revered traditional fieldwork but to complement it. There's undeniable value in hands-on teaching and direct student interaction, but platforms like the AI-powered simulator provide a controlled setting for targeted skill development. All other courses have project-oriented fieldwork.

It's important to emphasize that using this technology is not merely a "game" but a simulation experience. Your engagements within the platform are not about "winning" or "scoring high" but about learning and understanding. I am personally navigating the simulation modules, and not every interaction yields perfect results. Instead, they offer insights, revealing areas for professional growth. They help me understand the dynamics of AI-powered observations.

For this term, the simulations continue to be an essential part of Course XYZ. The commitment includes ten hours to explore the various modules and five hours for your paper and reflection. I encourage you to approach this as a learning opportunity and share your experiences, which can help inform our future curriculum decisions.

If you need guidance with the simulations or the platform, or have further queries, please do reach out. We have drop-in office hours on Monday. My aim is to ensure that your academic journey is both meaningful and supportive.

Warm regards,
Dr. Smith

Dr. Smith then followed up with several synchronous coaching sessions she called "simHuddles" and Debriefings, where the teacher candidates could show their simulation spaces via screen-sharing during video conferences and discuss their issues with peers and with Dr. Smith as a guide.

Questions for Discussion

1. How can educators effectively communicate the value of AI-enhanced teaching methods to skeptical students, as seen in the conflict between Dr. Smith and her students regarding using simulations?

2. In what ways does the introduction of AI in teacher training impact the professional independence of future educators, and how should this aspect be balanced with the need for technological readiness?
3. In what ways might AI in teacher training inadvertently perpetuate or amplify existing educational inequalities, and how can such risks be mitigated?
4. What role can ongoing feedback and support mechanisms play in mitigating student resistance and ensuring successful technology integration in higher education?
5. How can higher education programs ensure that AI tools are used to complement rather than diminish the role of human judgment and personal interaction in teaching?
6. What measures can be implemented to ensure that any student in higher education is not only proficient in using AI tools but also a critical and ethical user of such technology?
7. As AI continues to advance, what ethical considerations should educators and institutions keep in mind when incorporating AI-powered tools into higher education student training, and how can these concerns be addressed effectively?

For Further Reading

Barshay, J. (2018, July 30). *How artificial intelligence could help teachers do a better job*. The Hechinger Report. https://hechingerreport.org/how-artificial-intelligence-could-help-teachers-do-a-better-job/

Langreo, L. (2023, May 10). Can AI do teacher observations and deliver PD? In some schools, it already does. *Education Week*. https://www.edweek.org/leadership/can-ai-do-teacher-observations-and-deliver-pd-in-some-schools-it-already-does/2023/05#:~:text=In%20Some%20Schools%2C%20It%20Already%20Does,-By%20Lauraine%20Langreo&text=The%20Spokane%20school%20district%20in,and%20strengthen%20their%20classroom%20practices.

THIRTY-ONE

Video Dilemma: FERPA, Title IX, and Faculty Oversight

Shmuel Fink

AREAS FOR REFLECTION

- Faculty and student privacy rights
- Supervision of faculty
- Technology's impact on instructional practice

The Context

THE KEY PLAYERS IN ANY university are the faculty and students. Running a large department with a great number of faculty members is a challenge faced by department chairs in today's universities. Maintaining a good working relationship with the faculty is essential to the smooth running of the department. Faculty handbooks and policies help set up a structure that defines the parameters of that relationship. However, students are the main customers of the university. University policies are designed to revolve around what is best for their education. There are also government policies protecting rights, such as students' right to privacy. The goal of any university is to do what is best for both faculty and students.

The COVID-19 pandemic turned the world on its head and upended many policies. The face of education was forever changed. This posed challenges to all involved in higher education. What happens when your two main goals collide? What happens when student protection or privacy is at the expense of maintaining the faculty relationship or vice versa? How would such a scenario play out, and how can it best be resolved? This case study will focus on one such scenario.

COVID-19 completely changed the landscape of higher education. In spring 2020, 90% of higher education institutions in the United States cancelled in-person instruction and shifted to emergency remote teaching due to the COVID-19 pandemic (Lederman, 2020). A survey was conducted by Bay View Analytics, in collaboration with the Online Learning Consortium,

WICHE Cooperative for Educational Technologies, the University of Professional and Continuing Education Association, the Canadian Digital Learning Research Association, Cengage, and Every Learner Everywhere to determine the scope and effect of this transition. The study surveyed 826 faculty members and administrators at 641 American colleges and universities (Lederman, 2020).

The study indicates that over 90% of the institutions surveyed engaged in some form of emergency distance/virtual education to conduct or complete the spring term in 2020 (see Figure 31.1). Similarly, 76% of instructors reported that they had to move some of their courses online to complete the term. When asked to list the techniques they used to transition their courses to virtual settings, 80% of instructors cited utilizing synchronous video technology. Smaller proportions, but still the majority, used other forms of video. A total of 65% recorded their own lectures, and 51% said they used videos from third-party sources (Bay View Analytics, 2020). Many classes that were taught virtually were also recorded by the instructors to help students review, or as a way for students to access course content if they had missed a class.

Colleges were now faced with a dilemma. Course recordings, online proctoring, virtual sessions, and more are covered by FERPA (Family Educational Rights and Privacy Act) which provides certain rights related to educational

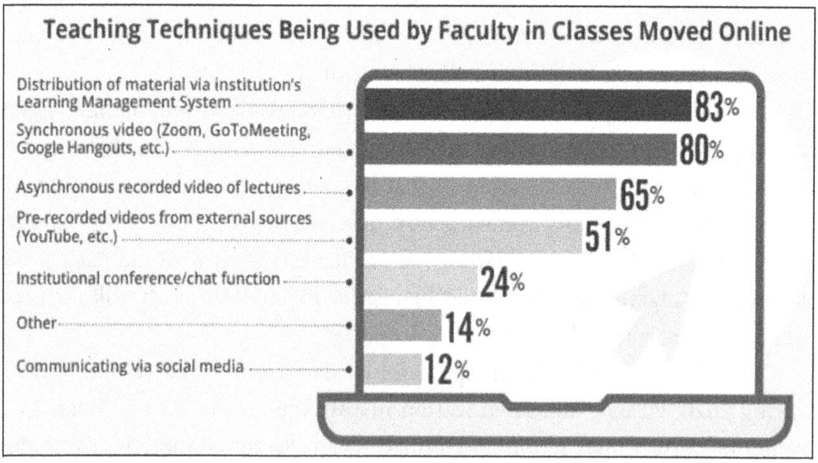

Figure 31.1. Teaching techniques being used by faculty in classes moved online. (Bay View Analytics, 2020)

records. Recorded classes are subject to FERPA protections in the same ways that traditional classes are covered if the video recording contains recordings of students. These videos then become "education records" (U.S. Department of Education, n.d.). Colleges and universities, therefore, had to formulate strict policies regarding the protection of these videos. One such policy stated by several colleges was that "[t]he University will not make use of these recordings for any purposes such as evaluation of instruction, investigating allegations of misconduct, or other non-instructional purposes" (Fordham, n.d.).

This policy also mitigated some of the fear instructors had in allowing classes to be recorded. Although the transition to virtual teaching was unavoidable, recording class sessions was not an absolute necessity. However, virtual teaching made it simple to record class sessions with a simple push of a button. In a study of 148 undergraduate students from a liberal arts college in Maine, students were asked to rate their level of agreement on a scale of 1 to 5, with preferences regarding classes held in a virtual environment, with 1 being "strongly disagree" and 5 being "strongly agree." The statement, "I prefer that lectures be recorded so that I can view them at my leisure," was rated at 4.21. Video recordings seemed to be important to the students (Murphy et al., 2020).

Many institutions, therefore, asked their professors to record their virtual sessions. Teachers were very reluctant. Not only were they being asked to use a technology that was new to them, but they were being asked to record themselves, as well. Some felt they were being put under a microscope, enabling the administration to observe any or all of their lectures at any time without notice. To alleviate this concern, colleges offered assurances that the recordings would not be employed for evaluation purposes. This assurance played a key role in assuaging reservations. Once instructors knew that these videos could not be used to evaluate them, they were more comfortable recording their virtual sessions, making this resource accessible to their students.

Professor Walter Niel was a professor of biology during this critical time. Although he was not formally trained in technology, he made the transition to teaching virtually along with all his fellow colleagues at Veridian University. As per university policy, all his virtual sessions were recorded and uploaded into the Learning Management System (LMS), Canvas. This LMS predated COVID-19. Every course taught at Veridian automatically has a Canvas "course" generated for it. Before COVID-19, the LMS was primarily used to facilitate the uploading of syllabi, posting announcements, and in some rare cases, posting homework assignments and managing grades.

With the advent of the pandemic, professors began to use the LMS much more regularly. Only the instructor and enrolled students have access to the course content, so uploading course videos to the LMS would be FERPA compliant. In many institutions, including Veridian University, it is common practice for department chairs to be added to all the Canvas courses offered in their department. This access enables them to review course activity and to ensure academic continuity.

In April of 2021, while courses were still being taught virtually and being recorded, Professor Niel's wife was involved in a car accident and sustained severe injuries. It became clear that she would need multiple emergency surgeries, necessitating that Professor Niel would miss at least the next few classes. The department chair, Dr. Adams, needed to hire a substitute to fill in for these classes. Dr. Adams felt that it would be insensitive to disturb Professor Niel and ask him what the class was up to while he was preoccupied with his wife and her serious medical condition. Instead, she opted to view the course video recording of the last lesson taught. Unbeknownst to her, this decision would propel her into a vortex of conflicting ethical considerations.

While viewing the course video, she noticed some inappropriate behavior on the part of the professor that she felt might constitute a Title IX violation, particularly focused on one student. In June 1972, President Nixon signed Title IX of the Education Amendments of 1972 into law. Title IX is a comprehensive federal law that has removed barriers that once prevented people, based on sex, from participating in educational opportunities and careers of their choice. It states that:

> No person in the United States shall, on the basis of sex, be excluded from participation in, be denied the benefits of, or be subjected to discrimination under any education program or activity receiving Federal financial assistance. (U.S. Department of Justice Civil Rights Division, n.d.)

Title IX protects students from sexual harassment in educational programs or activities operated by recipients of federal funding. The protection against sexual harassment derives from the general prohibitions against sex discrimination contained in the Title IX common rule. In addition, Title IX requires the college to take remedial action to overcome the effects of the discrimination. In its Code of Federal Regulations in common rule 1253.110 entitled "Remedial and affirmative action and self-evaluation," it explicitly states:

> *Remedial action.* If the designated agency official finds that a recipient has discriminated against persons on the basis of sex in an education program or activity, such recipient shall take such remedial action as the designated agency official deems necessary to overcome the effects of such discrimination. (U.S. Department of Justice Civil Rights Division, n.d.)

The Conflict/Challenge

Because Dr. Adams was concerned that there was a Title IX violation, she immediately turned the video over to the Regulatory Compliance Officer and Title IX Coordinator in the Office of Institutional Compliance (OIC). After reviewing the video, OIC got back to Dr. Adams to explain that, while the law had not strictly been violated, Professor Niel's behavior was not acceptable and was likely to be found objectionable by his students. The Regulatory Compliance Officer told Dr. Adams that this was a Human Resources issue, not a legal issue.

Dr. Adams now found herself faced with a dilemma. As per the University's COVID-19 policy, the video could not be used for faculty evaluation. However, remedial action was clearly required and is being recommended. Even under the best of circumstances, if this policy did not exist, this would be a sensitive and difficult conversation for Dr. Adams to have with Professor Niel.

Should she wait to see if the student filed a formal complaint? Maybe the student would not file such a grievance until she saw her grade after the semester. Even if a complaint was never filed, what about the future? If Dr. Adams did not speak to Professor Niel before he resumed teaching his classes, what would prevent this from happening again in the future? There was more than one incident in the one class session Dr. Adams viewed. It would certainly happen again. Dr. Adams could schedule a formal observation of an upcoming class, but she was confident he would not speak to students this way while she was observing the class. She knew he had never done so during prior observations.

In addition, perhaps there is now a need to review video recordings from other class sessions, as well. There may be statements Professor Niel made in other class sessions that did cross the Title IX line. In fact, according to NBC news, this phenomenon is not so uncommon (Burke, 2021). Post-COVID-19, there have been multiple cases of teachers and educators being caught on video making offensive, and often racist, comments. Given the reliance on video technology during the pandemic, "it's exposing what has been there," said Raechele Pope, Chief Diversity Officer for the University of Buffalo's Graduate School of Education. These video recordings provide an excellent window into the classroom and an opportunity to prevent future recurrences (Burke, 2021). This, however, would obviously directly undermine the University policy and its original intent. While inadvertently stumbling upon inappropriate comments when checking to see what the class was up to is one scenario, initiating an investigation of additional class recordings is an entirely different matter.

Questions for Discussion

1. Given that instructors were unwilling to record their virtual classes, what choices did the University have to ensure students could fully access their courses?
2. Under the circumstances, should Dr. Adams have viewed the video without Professor Niel's knowledge?
3. After seeing the video and receiving feedback from other offices, what, if anything, should Dr. Adams do?
4. Post-COVID-19, should instructors teaching virtually be required to record classes? If so, what should the University policy be regarding using those videos for faculty evaluation?
5. How does the potential harm to students from inappropriate behavior outweigh the privacy concerns of recording use?
6. What is the potential for a slippery slope if exceptions are made to the policy in cases of urgent issues?
7. What can universities do to balance Title IX enforcement and student safety while respecting existing policies to address faculty concerns?

8. Have you ever faced a similar dilemma? How did you handle the situation? What were the outcomes? How might those outcomes inform Dr. Adams' decision?
9. How can institutions balance the need for academic oversight with respecting the privacy of instructors and students?
10. How might institutions need to update their policies considering the growing reliance on technology for teaching and learning?

References

Bay View Analytics. (2020). *Pulse survey.* https://www.bayviewanalytics.com/reports/pulse/infographic-spring2020.pdf

Burke, M. (2021, April 26). *Zoom fails: Virtual classrooms expose teachers' racist, offensive rants.* NBC News. https://www.nbcnews.com/news/us-news/zoom-fails-virtual-classrooms-expose-teachers-racist-offensive-rants-n1264689

Fordham University. (n.d.). *Class recording notice and related policy.* https://www.fordham.edu/resources/policies/family-educational-rights-and-privacy-act-ferpa-policy/class-recording-notice-and-related-policy/

Lederman, D. (2020). *How teaching changed in the (forced) shift to remote learning: How professors changed their teaching in this spring's shift to remote learning.* Inside Higher Ed. https://www.insidehighered.com/digital-learning/article/2020/04/22/how-professors-changed-their-teaching-springs-shift-remote

Murphy, L., Eduljee, N. B., & Croteau, K. (2020). College student transition to synchronous virtual classes during the COVID-19 pandemic in Northeastern United States. *Pedagogical Research, 5*(4), 1–10. https://files.eric.ed.gov/fulltext/EJ1275517.pdf

Teachers College Columbia University. (n.d.). *Class Recording Policy.* Teachers College Policy Library. https://www.tc.columbia.edu/policylibrary/policies/class-recording-policy-11318300/

U.S. Department of Education. (n.d.). *FAQs on Photos and Videos under FERPA.* Protecting Student Privacy. https://studentprivacy.ed.gov/faq/faqs-photos-and-videos-under-ferpa

U.S. Department of Justice Civil Rights Division. (n.d.). *Title IX.* Title IX Legal Manual. https://www.justice.gov/crt/title-ix#I.%20Overview%20of%20Title%20IX:%20Interplay%20with%20Title%20VI,%20Section%20504,%20Title%20VII,%20and%20the%20Fourteenth%20Amendment

THIRTY-TWO

AI Assistant at the Meeting: A Clash of Privacy and Participation

Laurie Bobley

AREAS FOR REFLECTION

- Implementation of new technologies
- Ethical considerations
- Privacy rights

The Context

PROFESSOR JOHN HAWTHORNE IS A political science and history professor in the undergraduate department at Evergreen State College, a large public liberal arts institution in the southwestern part of the United States. The College has a large, renowned Political Science Department with 11 full-time faculty and 16 adjuncts. Professor Hawthorne is politely outspoken and friendly and stands out among his colleagues because he is always seeking to try new technologies for teaching and learning. He prides himself on keeping current with these tools, and often tries to help his colleagues integrate more technologies into their courses.

He was excited when Google Earth first came out and he quickly began to show his students maps of countries via satellite. He then taught them to find points that corresponded to important global political events so that they could appreciate the interrelatedness of these locations and recognize the proximity and significance of topographical features that often influence political decisions. He required students to create presentations using VoiceThread and Prezi when most of his colleagues across the college were still learning how to add audio to a PowerPoint presentation. He also was an early user of various tools to help facilitate group learning. When social annotation tools became available, he employed them to help students take notes and actively read and comment on complex course readings. As was typical, some students liked learning how to use these tools, but others were not happy and complained in course evaluations that they should not learn a new technology and new content simultaneously. Sometimes they asked why they had to learn how to use the tools at all, and commented, "I will never use this again."

When generative AI blasted into the mainstream of academia, Professor Hawthorne was the first to jump on the bandwagon as an early adopter. He quickly used it to assist him in reviewing rubrics and for suggesting revisions to his syllabi. He designed new assignments that students were required to use AI to complete. For example, in some of his assignments students would ask an AI Assistant to answer a specific challenging question or provide cogent points for one side of a debate. Students then needed to clearly show that they verified and corrected the content, after fact-checking what AI produced. They also needed to provide a verified list of references in proper MLA citation style. Finally, they conducted an error analysis for grammar and repetitiveness to further develop their writing skills. These annotations and comments were made directly on the AI generated document and uploaded to the Learning Management System.

When Professor Hawthorne heard about the growing range of AI Meeting Assistants that could record audio, produce written transcripts of virtual meetings, and capture slides, he became very excited. As he explored the growing array of these tools, he began to try them in his video conference lectures. He found that one tool made excellent transcripts of the entire online meeting, provided highlights and a short summary, and even outlined action items.

The Challenge/Conflict

Professor Hawthorne soon began using his AI Assistant at the monthly virtual faculty and committee meetings he attended. Any meeting scheduled on his calendar automatically triggered the AI Assistant to join the meeting, even before Professor Hawthorne did. It also remained at the meeting until the meeting ended, with or without Professor Hawthorne present. The Assistant was always there, recording, and Professor Hawthorne always shared the notes and recordings of the meetings with those on the meeting invitation. More than once, his immediate supervisor mentioned that he liked the transcription and believed that this tool was quite helpful as a recorder of the meeting minutes.

At first, the AI Assistant was innocuous, and everyone in the meetings basically ignored or accepted it. However, over a short period of time, meeting attendees started complaining about it to one another. Some said that they were uncomfortable, because as is typical before the start of a meeting, attendees might talk about personal or work-related happenings that they might not want recorded. A few weeks after the Assistant became "part of the team," some tech savvy faculty members who were hosting meetings realized that just as they could remove any participant from the meeting, they could also remove the Assistant. Meeting hosts then began to remove it before Professor Hawthorne arrived. Professor Hawthorne protested after one meeting that he did not attend, saying that he did not have the valuable notes he needed. During a virtual meeting, one faculty member casually complained to the chairperson about the use of the Assistant. The chairperson responded, "We need to step into the 21st century and embrace AI as a tool that will certainly be in our daily lives."

The chairperson discussed the complaint with Professor Hawthorne, who argued that if he were present, he would be taking notes anyway. Not allowing the AI Assistant at a meeting restricted his ability to participate fully in meetings. He continued to argue that it was simply like another person being at the meeting—if someone had something private to say and did not want to say it in front of Professor Hawthorne, they shouldn't have said it in front of his Assistant. A few of the faculty felt that this was an invasion of privacy, but the chairperson did not agree. Her response echoed what Professor Hawthorne said: "It's, like, if there's something you don't want to say in front of him or others, you shouldn't say it in front of his AI Assistant." A small group decided to bring the issue to the dean.

Questions for Discussion

1. How should the chairperson have reacted when faculty were complaining, even though she agreed with Professor Hawthorne?
2. What ethical considerations are involved in this situation?
3. What privacy issues might be violated by using this tool in meetings?
4. After receiving this complaint, what should the dean do?
5. While waiting for a decision from the dean, what actions can be taken by faculty who don't like the AI Assistant in meetings?

6. Would an issue such as this be a department- or college-wide policy decision, and why?

For Further Reading

Kine. P. (2022, February 16). *My journey down the rabbit hole of every journalist's favorite app.* Politico. https://www.politico.com/news/2022/02/16/my-journey-down-the-rabbit-hole-of-every-journalists-favorite-app-00009216

Vaughan-Nichols, S. (2023, August 9). *Zoom is entangled in an AI privacy mess.* ZDNET. https://www.zdnet.com/article/zoom-is-entangled-in-an-ai-privacy-mess/

PART VI

OVERCOMING PERFORMANCE ISSUES

THIRTY-THREE

New Leader, Hidden Problems

Sabra Brock

AREAS FOR REFLECTION

- Whistleblowing
- Challenging disciplinary actions
- Assistance and training for new chairs and supervisors

The Context

DESIRADA ELI WAS THE NEW chair of the 20-person Sociology Department at Towne College. She had been teaching in that department for two years, starting immediately after earning her Ph.D. The exiting chair had held the position for ten years and would continue working as a full-time faculty member.

Desirada was a popular choice with five other full-time faculty as she got off to a good start with a personal interview with each of them. She also was well-received by the 15 regular adjuncts. She asked for their ideas to improve the department and for growing the student body of a program that had been losing enrollment.

Her search to find the duties of a chairperson resulted in conflicting descriptions and incomplete information. When she asked the outgoing chair for guidance, he was cordial in conversation, but offered her no real background on her new position as a chairperson, saying she had worked for him for two years and should have absorbed enough. As the new semester approached, the course assignments she made were well-received, and she felt the department was off on a positive footing.

The Conflict/Challenge

Several weeks into the semester, the site coordinator who monitored faculty attendance for each class phoned Desirada and informed her that several students reported that the professor for the Sociology 101 class had appeared intoxicated. The site coordinator also noticed the impaired behavior when the professor checked in for his classes. He said it was not the first time he saw this faculty member appearing to be intoxicated. Desirada was surprised, as Joseph Deer had been an adjunct for several years at Towne College. His doctoral work was directly related to the course he was teaching, and there had been no other complaints reported that she knew of.

When she spoke with Professor Deer later that day, she asked him how things, in general, were going for him and, specifically, how this semester had started out. He reported a significant tragedy, as both of his parents had been killed that summer in an auto accident. He admitted being challenged but felt he was performing adequately in the classroom.

Desirada mentioned that several students had complained that he had appeared intoxicated during last night's class. He became belligerent and denied that this was the case. He did admit to taking prescription medicine prescribed by his psychotherapist while he worked through his grief. He demanded to know who had reported him. Desirada did not reveal the students' names but, when pressed, said that the site director had noticed the behavior, received the complaint, and reported the situation to her.

A class visit was set up for the following week. Desirada arrived in the classroom, Professor Deer was not present, but several students were. She introduced herself as the chair and indicated she occasionally likes to visit the classrooms of her faculty. Professor Deer came exactly at the hour the class was to begin. He did not appear to be intoxicated at the beginning of class, but as the hour went on, he stumbled repeatedly and then lost his train of thought several times. At the break, Desirada took him aside and said that her perception was that he did appear impaired and informed him that she would end the class early. She suggested that he give a larger than usual homework assignment to make up for the missed classroom time, and he agreed.

The next day, Desirada felt sufficiently concerned to bring up the incident with the dean of faculty. He revealed that there had in fact been several complaints and observations of apparent intoxication involving this professor last year, but no formal complaints had been filed.

The dean decided to interview Professor Deer. He was met with the same belligerence and denial that Desirada had experienced. On further examination, more evidence of the professor's problem with alcohol emerged, so he was put on probation.

Desirada thought the case was closed until the dean called her into his office for a closed-door session. She had been reported as a "whistle-blower" for mentioning another employee as an observer of the apparent intoxication. This incident would be added into her permanent HR file. She found the following definition of a whistleblower: "A protected whistleblower is an employee who discloses a violation of any law, rule, or regulation; gross mismanagement; a gross waste of funds; an abuse of authority; or a substantial and specific danger to public health or safety" (Grundmann, 2010).

Questions for Discussion

1. Was Desirada unfairly punished for mentioning the site director's name as an observer of a faculty member's behavior?
2. On what basis could Desirada challenge the dean's disciplinary action?
3. What is the responsibility of a chairperson to assure that faculty members are behaving professionally?
4. When unprofessional behavior is reported, who should discipline the faculty member?
5. What are appropriate next steps when unprofessional behavior among faculty is reported by students?

Reference

Grundmann, S. T. (2010). *Whistleblower protections for federal employees citing Title 5 US State Code § 2302(b)(8)*. U.S. Merit Systems Protection Board. https://www.mspb.gov/studies/studies/Whistleblower_Protections_for_Federal_Employees_557972.pdf

THIRTY-FOUR

The Professor's Academic Dilemma

Kenneth S. Bigel

AREAS FOR REFLECTION

- Mentoring
- Academic integrity
- Scholarly publication standards

The Context

An undergraduate student, "George," wishes to improve his chances for acceptance to an elite graduate school. He communicates his desire to work on a research project with the most prominent scholar in the department in which he majors. He is sincere and wants desperately to get ahead.

The professor responds, indicating that he has no appropriate work for the student presently, and that he usually works with graduate students. He asks George whether he has had any courses in advanced statistics, research methods, or in writing research papers. George admits that he is not at all skilled in these areas and has had no coursework in these areas. The professor refers the student to a professor at another university who may be able to work with him to boost these necessary skills.

When approached by George, the professor from the other university informs him that his free time is scarce, but that he would be willing to work with him outside the aegis of his university for a fee, so that George could acquire some basic key skills. The professor makes it clear that this would be "extra-curricular" and in no way connected to his university. They would identify a topic of interest, structure a review of the literature, conduct research, and then write a paper. The professor indicated that when applying for graduate school, George could use the paper as an example of something he had written in collaboration with a professor. As the paper is intended as a research project, it might later be published. In either event, George would have to acknowledge in the paper that he worked with said professor, including the professor's name either in the byline or in an acknowledgment section.

During the following three months, George and the professor worked well together and completed the paper. In the interim, George worked quite hard and acquired many skills emanating from the professor's dedicated tutelage. George thanked the professor for his assistance. He could never have accomplished what he did without the professor. He then pays the professor.

The Conflict/Challenge

Approximately ten months later, the professor receives an email from George requesting that he write a letter of recommendation for graduate school. While getting reacquainted, the professor asks for George's final draft of the paper. George sends a link to his paper, now published in a secondary for-fee journal. The professor notes that there is no acknowledgment of the professor's contribution.

In a follow-up conversation, the professor points out that George should have acknowledged any assistance that he received from him or elsewhere, including that of a paid editor about whom George disclosed in a prior conversation. Not doing so makes it appear that he wrote a paper that is beyond his true skill level and thus constitutes a form of plagiarism and a violation of academic integrity. George initially says that the online publication submission format did not allow him to enter two names in the byline; later he states that he "forgot" to do so.

The professor debates whether he should write the letter of recommendation. The letter will not be accessible to the student. Should he include the plagiarism detail in the letter? The student had been intelligent, diligent, and respectful throughout their prior dealings and relationship.

Questions for Discussion

1. If the plagiarism is disclosed, what actions can be taken against the student by the journal, one of the two colleges, or a professional organization, if any?
2. Is there a tacit commitment by the professor, to the student, to write a letter of recommendation? Why or why not?

3. As the professor ponders writing a letter of recommendation, should he or should he not include information about the plagiarism? Explain
4. How might the professor's own ethics and integrity be compromised by writing the letter of recommendation without disclosing the plagiarism?
5. What steps can the professor take to ensure that other students he may work with fully understand the meaning of plagiarism and academic integrity, and the ramifications of not adhering to widely held expectations related to writing and professional conduct?

THIRTY-FIVE

Unveiling the Underperformer: Addressing New Employee Performance Challenges

Laurie Bobley

AREAS FOR REFLECTION

- Human Resources processes
- Assessing applicant skills
- Onboarding new employees

The Context

TONI, THE NEW PROGRAM ASSOCIATE, was not the first choice of the hiring committee. There had been pressure to hire someone relatively quickly because the position would be vacant in less than a week, and applications for admission would begin to flood into the office soon after. In the past, jobs were left unfilled for substantial periods of time because the hiring process took so long that the qualified applicants accepted positions elsewhere. The process involved video conference interviews for the first round. Finalists were invited to campus for in-person interviews with the hiring committee and other relevant staff. As a final step, each interviewee would provide a writing sample before leaving campus.

The applicant pool for this position was small. Even so, reviewing applications and scheduling and conducting interviews with five applicants took almost three weeks. The first applicant interviewed was also the first choice, and as soon as all interviews were complete, he was offered the position by the chairperson. He thanked the chairperson but informed him that he could not accept the job because he had received another offer which he had accepted a few days earlier. The second choice was then contacted. She returned the call immediately and stated that she could not accept the position. At this point, it was nearing a month from the time that the interviews were concluded. The hiring committee checked to see if there were any new applications, which there were, but none of the applicants seemed to be a good fit.

The third choice, Toni, did not fully meet all the qualifications of the position, but because of the need for immediate help in the department, and the fact that there were no new applicants, she was contacted. It took almost one week for her to reply to the phone call and follow-up email. Although that did seem odd, she was offered the job, accepted, and began work a few weeks later.

Toni had a quiet, easygoing, pleasant personality, and she seemed eager to learn. However, after a few weeks, her immediate supervisor Alyce complained that Toni was very slow to learn many simple tasks, and those that she should know how to do were taking much longer to complete than they should. She noted that tasks such as accurate checking of lists, completing forms correctly, contacting the correct students, creating and populating spreadsheets, and filling in and sending template emails are basic office tasks, and anyone should be able to complete these quickly and efficiently within a few days of starting a new job. Alyce corrects Toni when she sees mistakes, but Toni seems to continue to repeat them.

During the first month of employment, Toni took two days of sick leave on two different days. In the second month, Toni took another two sick days and called in one day saying that she would be late because she had an appointment with a doctor that she forgot about. At one point she asked when she could take her first vacation day.

The work schedule allowed employees to work remotely two days each week. Once, when Toni was working from home, Alyce asked to meet through video conference, but Toni said that she had spotty Internet and did not have reliable access to video conferencing at home. She also said her computer was a bit old. They met anyway and completed the meeting without any disruptions. In month three, on a day that Toni was supposed to report to work, she told Alyce that she was sick but could work from home. Alyce emailed Toni to ask her to meet online. About an hour later, Toni responded that she could meet, and they both logged into the online meeting room. Alyce immediately noticed that Toni was wearing a blanket draped around her, indicating that she may have been cold, but as the meeting progressed, she also noticed that Toni looked exceptionally put together. She seemed to have a lot of make-up on, and she was wearing large, shiny earrings. After the meeting ended, Alyce thought that Toni does not normally look that good at work, and earrings like that are generally something worn when going out, not while at home when you're ill.

When Alyce told a colleague about the mounting number of issues with this new employee, the colleague mentioned that she saw Toni walking through the hallway and heard her on the phone telling someone that she "needed many more hours next month." Because Toni's job was a salaried position, and she was not paid hourly, they wondered whether Toni had another job elsewhere.

The Conflict/Challenge

On the job, as time passes, Toni continues to make many mistakes and is very slow to learn. However, she does seem to try to learn: She asks many questions to help her better understand her responsibilities and the tasks she must complete. Toni has also been taking fewer sick days and seems to like the job. Alyce has explored the process of terminating Toni, yet she feels uncomfortable and unsure about pursuing that option.

It's time for the annual staff review. Even though Toni has been on the job only a few months, Alyce thinks she should meet with her but does not know how to approach the meeting. Alyce does not believe that Toni is right for the job but feels bad about taking steps to fire her.

Questions for Discussion

1. How can applicant competencies be determined during the interview process?
2. What should a supervisor include in initial discussions when onboarding a new employee?
3. After hiring, what steps should the supervisor take to prepare the new hire to fulfill the responsibilities of the position?
4. When a manager identifies employee deficiencies, what actions should be taken? How would this differ for new employees?
5. How long should a supervisor tolerate deficiencies before taking actions to terminate?
6. In this case, what ethical issues might exist on the part of the manager or the employee?
7. What is the best way to monitor employees who work remotely?

THIRTY-SIX

What Higher Education Can Learn About Employee Burnout from the Hospitality Industry

Gena Bardwell

AREAS FOR REFLECTION

- Human Resources processes
- Employee rights
- Supervisor/manager training on social-emotional health

The Context

THE HOTEL INDUSTRY BY ITS very nature is all about customer service and hospitality. This midwestern property is a bustling 4-star convention hotel which stays filled 76% of the year. It has two major money-making divisions: rooms and food and beverage. Conference rooms are sold by a team of sales staff and supervised by the director of sales. Reservations personnel assist in booking conference block room sales and managing individual sales, which are separate from meetings or conferences. Rooms are cleaned, sanitized, and replenished with amenities by housekeeping staff supervised by the director of housekeeping. Conference logistics are managed by a team of convention services staff under the guidance and supervision of the director of convention services. A convention services manager also works directly with the banquet manager and chef to plan conference meals and coffee breaks. Restaurants, lounges, gift stores, and exercise spaces are assigned managers who each report to someone more senior in their division. It is important to note that there is a lot of collaboration among departments within any hotel as it relates to filling the need of organizations hosting conferences at the property.

Managers and directors seek to deliver better-than-satisfactory service to customers and clients on a grand scale, which is ultimately important to an organization's brand and financial success. Leaders, however, often fail to see the toll that great service takes on rank and file or supervisory employees over time. This is especially important to consider when an incident occurs outside the norm and requires problem-solving, deep listening, and interpersonal communication skills to help a worker execute, navigate, and/or complete tasks more efficiently.

Mary is a nine-year employee and staff supervisor in the hotel's food and beverage division. She helps with logistics and provides support wherever needed. During the last two years, her role was managing supervisor of over 20 staff members. She worked hard and was respected by her staff. No job was too low, and she would often pitch in when necessary. Mary's boss frowned on her "can do anything" attitude. He thought it made her staff too dependent on her and less able to perform their own jobs effectively.

Mary also had domestic problems. Her fiancé would wait for her at work each evening and drive her home. Mary dreaded the silence between them as much as the arguing. He often accused her of incidents that had not happened, and even presented evidence that seemingly indicated that they did occur. She was concerned that the tension was beginning to affect her job performance.

Right before a three-day weekend, she learned that a theft had taken place in her division, which triggered a security issue.

The Conflict/Challenge

On Tuesday morning Mary was called into her supervisor's office for questioning. Mary had never been reprimanded for anything and was not expecting that she would be this time either. In fact, she thought she and her supervisor would be talking about the change in her schedule that she had requested over a month ago.

Instead, when she sat down, the supervisor told her that some of her inventory had come up short. The boss showed her a box of items that were identified as taken from her department; these had been delivered to the security department early that morning. Mary admitted that the items seemed to be from her department. Confused, Mary asked for clarification about the details. Mary's boss said a gentleman claiming to be Mary's fiancé said that Mary took the items from the storeroom and brought them home. He said he could not live with himself knowing stolen goods were in the house, so he returned them. Mary was in a state of shock. Being a very private person, Mary never discussed her domestic problems at work. She now felt that she had to reveal that the verbal and emotional abuse from her fiancé made her fearful. She also stated that her fiancé had been gaslighting her by claiming incidents of "stolen items" that were not true.

The supervisor was confronted with conflicting information. Mary was a valued employee: she potentially committed a crime, or she may have been falsely accused of theft by her fiancé. Mary asks, "Are you firing me?"

Noting how stressed Mary was, he responded, "I don't know. I am not sure. Right now, I need to review all my options. You may go back to work or go home. I will leave the choice up to you, but do not discuss this with anyone. I will get back to you as quickly as possible."

As was Mary's nature, she believed that she had no choice but to stay at work and complete her schedule for the week. "There is no one who can do this job but me." Mary returned to her office in a state of bewilderment but knew she needed to wait for the final decision.

Questions for Discussion

1. How might the lessons in this case relate to higher education?
2. Considering the evidence presented, was Mary's boss correct to take time before deciding next steps, and why?
3. While taking time to decide about Mary's future at the hotel, and recognizing her emotional distress, what should the supervisor do next?
4. How do leaders identify what needs to be done first, then once identified, prioritize their action steps?
5. How should leaders be trained to recognize emotional distress or burnout?
6. What are some best practices for training leaders in interpersonal communication and empathy?

PART VII

PROFESSIONAL GROWTH

THIRTY-SEVEN

Faculty Development from the Top Down or Bottom Up?

Carrie DiMatteo

AREAS FOR REFLECTION

- Faculty development
- Value of stakeholder input
- Professional growth

The Context

Big Bear University has a central campus in a large metropolitan area with satellite campuses around the country and the world. The University includes undergraduate, graduate, and professional programs, including Law and Medical Schools. The University does not award tenure to its faculty, but faculty can be promoted based on excellence in scholarship, teaching, and service.

Several years ago, the University established a Faculty Development Center (FDC), which is centrally administered under the Provost's Office and hosts workshops related to teaching in higher education. These workshops are available to all full-time and adjunct faculty at the University.

Despite a large faculty roster at the University, workshops hosted by the FDC have had low enrollment. Because many faculty work at campuses far from the University's central campus, nearly all FDC events have been held exclusively online. Additionally, there is no central physical location.

The FDC's budget allows for a single paid director who divides her time between the FDC and other administrative responsibilities in the Provost's Office. The FDC's director works alone, except when seeking approval from the provost. Some faculty at Big Bear University have wondered if the FDC operates without enough of a bottom-up, faculty-led approach. Several faculty members have been asked to contribute to operations related to the FDC as a component of their service to the University, but their work is not compensated, nor has it been formally recognized.

Beyond the organizational challenge of how to provide effective faculty development is a more personal conflict facing faculty: wanting to receive faculty development while feeling increasingly "burned out" by the number of meetings to attend and the number of contributions they are asked to make for service, which factors less into promotion decisions.

The primary stakeholders of faculty development are faculty, of whom there are at least two types: those desiring more and better faculty development, and those not wishing to do any more than the minimum requirement of their jobs. Above the faculty are administrative leaders, who want an optimized faculty. Below the faculty are students, who will reap the greatest rewards from a more developed faculty.

The Conflict/Challenge

To increase faculty participation in FDC events, the FDC director has initiated additional FDC events—weekly meetings which are facilitated by a guest speaker from within the University who is carefully vetted and approved by the provost. Despite having more frequent faculty development events, attendance has remained low. Those faculty not wishing to attend still do not, and those faculty wanting more and better faculty development still crave more, including a physical location in which to gather, and events that feel carefully tailored to them.

An alternative approach to faculty development, which has been taken up by some faculty members, is to gather informally to talk about issues related to teaching in higher education. These smaller and more informal faculty gatherings have been particularly helpful in creating feelings of camaraderie and belonging among faculty attendees. This bottom-up approach seems to work well for those who have initiated it, but is it ideal for everyone? Several faculty leaders have discussed presenting this alternative approach to the FDC director and/or the provost.

Questions for Discussion

1. What next steps should these faculty leaders take?
2. What are the potential drawbacks or limitations of this alternative approach?

3. What could be done to implement a more bottom-up or informal approach to faculty development as part of a university-wide offering?
4. If unsuccessful in convincing the administration to implement their alternative approach to faculty development, should these leaders create and provide informal training opportunities for their own faculty peers?
5. What are the risks and benefits of faculty presenting their ideas to the provost directly?
6. Who is better equipped to provide faculty development opportunities: the organization or the faculty?
7. How do the size and spread of a university's campuses impact how faculty development is provided?

THIRTY-EIGHT

Preparing for the Workplace

Sabra Brock

AREAS FOR REFLECTION

- Third-party programs as educational tools
- Internships
- Potential employer relationships

The Context

Australia Technology University (ATU) is a premier college in Sydney known for innovative curriculum and strong relationships with local and global industries. There is rightful pride in the many internship programs they supervise in metropolitan Sydney and abroad.

Jillian Brown is the founder of a web platform with a mission of providing positive news in an engaging format. When she founded it eight years ago, she believed that the world needed more "cheerscrolling" to counteract the "doomscrolling" of negative news so prevalent in today's media. Since its inception, the platform has attracted more than 7,000 ideas over a range of categories including fintech, dining, and artistic ideas. A group of 12 editors supervises each category and post with a visual and a description of no more than 100 words.

Largely self-funded, Jillian depends on generating development ideas for the platform that are free or low-cost. Therefore, she was excited when Ralph Osgood from ATU reached out to her asking if she would sponsor a team of five interns for the spring semester. Each intern would have a faculty supervisor and be required to submit specific deliverables connecting the workplace experience with the University curriculum. Ralph, as chair of the Business Department, would serve as the faculty supervisor.

The Conflict/Challenge

As the semester takes shape, Jillian submits a job description for each intern team member. Each would be evaluating the platform for appeal and possible usage from the millennial generation point-of-view. The evaluations would lead to suggestions for modifications.

Jillian spent time crafting her expectations for the interns, reviewing them with Ralph, and presenting them to the five interns at the start of their semester. She thought that the students understood the directive and appreciated their enthusiasm at undertaking the project.

However, when Jillian got the first report of their findings, she was disappointed that the reflections were superficial and did not appear to represent more than a cursory look at the site.

She knew she needed to address her concerns with Ralph; otherwise, the work with ATU would prove to be a complete waste of time.

Questions for Discussion

1. What should Jillian do to improve the usefulness of the intern work?
2. What additional guidelines could Jillian have put in place for intern work before the start of the semester?
3. Were there guidelines that the University could have put in place for intern work before the start of the semester?
4. What responsibility does the University supervisor have for assuring that the needs of the interns' employer are met?

THIRTY-NINE

Rejected, Not Defeated

Laurie Bobley, Sabra Brock, and Alan Sebel

AREAS FOR REFLECTION

- Perseverance
- Project development
- Hierarchy of leadership
- Succession planning

The Context

PREMIER UNIVERSITY IS AN UP-AND-COMING university that has recently celebrated its 35th anniversary. Growth has been rapid in enrollment and in acquiring a diverse group of colleges in several locations across the United States and internationally. The University was initially envisioned as an organization that emphasized excellent teaching, over research. A proven record in teaching excellence was generally a hiring criterion, but there was much variation in styles and quality of teaching across the 30-plus schools. It had recently began offering a formal professional development program for faculty to hone their teaching skills, which led to hiring several instructional designers.

Marie Caron had initially been hired as an assistant professor in Premier's Graduate School of Technology, but because of her exceptional teaching reviews and proficiency with instructional technology, she was offered the position of lead instructional designer, which she accepted. She soon began her doctoral degree in educational leadership at a university in a nearby metropolis. Part of the doctoral curriculum was an action research project: Each doctoral student identifies a challenge in higher education and spends several semesters researching it and developing a practical solution to address it. A gap that Marie identified in her own institution was that there seemed to be no clear path for faculty to be recognized and potentially promoted to higher-level administrative positions, such as director.

Conversations with faculty members during their training sessions confirmed Marie's impression about the lack of a path to assume greater leadership roles in the University. Some faculty members indicated that they were interested in moving up through the organization to positions of chairperson and eventually dean but did not know how they could start. Marie recognized that there was little opportunity to formally develop needed leadership skills. As in most institutions, faculty were identified for promotion by demonstrating the capacity for leadership through their willingness to take on administrative responsibilities beyond their teaching load, increased participation on committees, and resilience in the changing environment of the University. She also discovered that there was no budget for external training. Given this, she conceptualized a way to create an internal resource for faculty leadership development.

The Conflict/Challenge

Marie found that faculty leadership development programs were a model used in some of the more progressive universities. Once she finished her advanced degree, she spent the summer putting together a proposal for a faculty leadership training institute at Premier University. She reviewed the models from other universities and developed sample agendas for a nine-month structured leadership development program. Prior to bringing the idea to her dean, she shared her ideas with two trusted colleagues and made minor adjustments. Marie then requested an appointment with the dean.

The proposal presented to the dean included a summary of what other universities were doing, anecdotal information from her conversations with other faculty, and the identified need for succession planning. While she was presenting her idea to the dean, he was listening, but had a quizzical expression on his face. He wanted to know if perhaps administrative staff might feel slighted that they were not given the same chance to upskill and thus increase promotion chances. The dean had no other reaction, and at the end of the presentation, he thanked her and promised to think about her proposal and get back to her.

Marie asked politely when she might expect a response. He seemed a bit annoyed but promised an answer by the end of September. In early October, Marie still had not heard from him, so she sent him a gentle reminder. When the response came in mid-October, it was a short email indicating that her proposal, while interesting, would not be a priority for the coming budget year and perhaps not even the following years. In view of the rejection, Marie considered ways to get this program approved because the research she had done during her doctoral program indicated that this type of program would greatly benefit the University.

Questions for Discussion

1. Given the outcome of her proposal to the dean, what could Marie have done differently to achieve her goal of establishing a leadership development program?
2. What reasons other than the budget might the dean have had for rejecting the proposal?
3. What strategies would work to initiate a needed project when it has been rejected by an immediate supervisor?
4. What could the leadership of a university do to encourage ideas from the employees who might have solutions to problems leaders may not see?
5. What is the value of succession planning to a university?

FORTY

The Socratic Method in Mathematics Lectures

Marius Fahrner and Birgit Wolf

AREAS FOR REFLECTION

- Pedagogical choices
- Depth of learning vs. covering required content
- Professional growth

The Context

STUDENTS FROM VARIOUS DISCIPLINES NEED mathematical skills to be successful in their fields of study. To acquire relevant mathematical skills, students not majoring in mathematics are required to successfully pass selected mathematics lectures. As a rule, and among other grading components, a performance assessment in the form of a written exam is conducted at the end of the term; students not majoring in mathematics often struggle to pass these written examinations. One of the reasons why students then fail a mathematics course is that lack of prerequisite mathematical knowledge. Mathematics skills of freshman students very often vary significantly at the start of their studies. This is especially true at universities where students have acquired university entrance qualifications from different educational systems and countries, (e.g., a German Abitur, a United States high school Diploma, or an international baccalaureate). In addition to students' lack of competencies and knowledge, the systematic approach to solving challenging mathematical problems is very often not well-developed. For these students to understand complex mathematical issues, additional intermediate steps must be incorporated and developed in these basic mathematics lectures. Due to the students' lack of prior mathematical knowledge and insufficient methodological skills, teachers are faced with the question of whether there is a didactic teaching method that enables low-achieving students to develop their mathematical skills adequately. The Socratic method could be chosen as a suitable teaching method.

The Socratic method corresponds to the respective competence level of the students in the class. The individual problem is worked on, step-by-step in various intermediate steps, until the final solution to the problem becomes apparent. In addition, learners must work out the solution to the problem as independently as possible to promote their own skills in the medium and long term (Fahrner & Wolf, 2019; Freydberg, 2020; Wilberding, 2021).

Professor Wu teaches Mathematics 1 at Generalis University in the Department of Psychology. This course is compulsory and must be passed by all students. While some students are very enthusiastic about the course tasks, other students are frustrated by these tasks and the course in general. In addition to a lack of prior knowledge and insufficient methodological skills, a lack of motivation characterizes many students as they work to learn the content of the course. Some even complain that, given the fact that they are enrolled in a psychology program, they should not have to take a mathematics course. Professor Wu, therefore, has his work cut out for him. Not only does he have to deal with the different entry levels of the students, but he also needs to motivate students to participate seriously in the first place.

He is thrown in at the deep end in the very first lecture as he deals with a mathematical extreme value problem and wants to explain to the students how minima and maxima of functions can be determined. However, when he starts to calculate the first derivative of a function, he looks into astonished and sometimes annoyed faces. Displeasure spreads through the class; statements such as "I've never seen that before," "It's too abstract for me," and even, "It's too much for me and I'm already fed up" are made. Professor Wu must admit that he has to change his teaching methods if he wants to teach the students successfully. Fortunately, before the lecture, he had already considered the possibility that some students would have significant problems understanding mathematical facts. During the semester break, he read several books on didactic concepts in teaching mathematics that can be applied to learners with lower mathematical skills. He was particularly impressed by the Socratic method, which he now wants to apply. He begins with the "what-is" question, typical of a Socratic conversation—in this case, "What is a derivative?" Some students, working in groups, can answer this question collaboratively and explain the concept of the first derivative to their peers who lack understanding. The mood in the classroom changes immediately.

The frustration caused by a lack of understanding turns into curiosity. The students would now like to discuss the extreme value problem in more detail.

To help the students a little with their problem-solving, Professor Wu asks an open question, which is typical of a Socratic dialogue—in this case, "Is there a connection between the first derivative and the geometry of the curve?" After some detours and untrue statements, which could be identified as false statements by Professor Wu's Socratic-style questioning, a student makes the factual statement that the value of the derivative can be related to the slope of the curve.

Finally, students who were initially not interested in solving the extreme value problem but who had increased their motivation during the problem-solving process also spoke up. They concluded that there is a gradient of "0" at minima or maxima, so the first derivative must be "0" at such points. Professor Wu was satisfied with this result. He realized that his reading on didactic concepts during his lecture-free period had paid off. Not only was he able to get the already-interested students to solve a challenging mathematical problem on their own, but during the problem-solving process, he was even able to lead the less motivated students to a positive learning attitude and encourage them to cooperate. Even though teaching with the Socratic method is demanding, time-consuming, and exhausting, Professor Wu will continue to use the Socratic method as a didactic tool in his lessons in the future, due to the positive results.

The Conflict/Challenge

Although the Socratic method as a teaching method contributes significantly to the expansion of students' skills, some critical aspects must also be pointed out concerning the application of the Socratic method. The Socratic method requires a lot of time. The additional time allows the mathematical problems to be dealt with in depth; however, only a few issues can be discussed in a single lesson. There is a risk that many problems will remain unresolved if the Socratic method is used exclusively. Furthermore, when using the Socratic method, the constant questioning of statements demands a high level of concentration from both the students and the teacher. This can easily lead to excessive demands. It is, therefore, advisable not to use the Socratic method throughout the course, but only for a few specific problems. This ensures that students improve their mathematical skills without missing out on important topics or being overwhelmed.

Questions for Discussion

1. What guidelines should Professor Wu use to form collaborative groups to apply the Socratic method effectively?
2. How can students be motivated to work on mathematical problems or other coursework that they do not find applicable to their own lives or professions?
3. What other methods can be used to help students with a lack of foundational content knowledge succeed in their studies?
4. As an academic leader, how can you incentivize your faculty to selectively use the Socratic method?
5. How can you use the Socratic method in other instances, such as professional development?

References

Fahrner, M., & Wolf, B. (2019). Überfachlicher kompetenzerwerb durch anwendung der sokratischen methode in der mathematik. In T. Schmohl & D. Schäffer (Hrsg.), *Lehrexperimente der hochschulbildung: Didaktische innovationen aus den fächern* (Teaching Xchange, Bd. 2, vollst. überarb. U. erw. Neuaufl) (S. 99-116). Bielefeld: wbv.

Freydberg, B. (2020). The Socratic method, once and for all. *Comparative and Continental Philosophy, 12*(3), 240–244.

Wilberding, E. (2021). *Socratic methods in the classroom: Encouraging critical thinking and problem solving through dialogue.* New York.

About the Contributors

Gena Bardwell, M.F.A., is Director of General Education and Chair of the Department of Speech and Communication for Touro University NY (TUNY) undergraduate division. She received the prestigious Presidential Award for Service in 2022 from Dr. Kadish. She teaches Public Speaking, Event Management, Interpersonal Communication, and Human Communications. She hosts a TUNY podcast called *The Faculty Chronicles*. She has presented at TU's annual Assessment Summit and undergraduate Faculty Senate, and was a guest speaker on best communication practices for the Graduate School of Education, Graduate Council, and Doctoral Physical Therapy program. She formerly worked at Scholastic, Inc. as a Senior Manager in corporate communication.

Timothy Bellavia, M.F.A., is an award-winning children's author, fabric artist, and educator, and is an Assistant Professor at Touro University. He is known for the We Are All the Same Inside series of children's books. Professor Bellavia has collaborated with Sesame Workshop and several other non-profit organizations. He champions STEAM education and was part of a five-year research project funded by the United States Department of Education.

Ruth A. Best, Ed.D., M.B.A., became a New York City Teaching Fellow after a ten-year career in business. Her passion for teaching, staff development, and mentoring was the catalyst for her subsequent transition into higher education at Mercy University. In 2010, Dr. Best became the founding dean of Faculty Development and Instructional Design at The College of Westchester. She also contracted as a course developer and online group facilitator for graduate-level courses in management at the University of the West Indies, Open Campus. More recently, she has served as an assistant dean and faculty member in Touro University's Graduate School of Education.

Kenneth S. Bigel, Ph.D., M.B.A., C.F.P.®, is Professor of Finance and Business Ethics at Touro University. He is author, most recently, of *Introduction to Financial Analysis* (2022) and *Corporate Finance* (2023), both of which are available online through Pressbooks. His next text, *Fixed Income Mathematics*, is scheduled to be published in the last quarter of 2024. Dr. Bigel has also begun work on a monograph tentatively titled, *The Spirit of Judaism: A Deep Dive into Jewish Virtue Ethics*.

Laurie Bobley, Ed.D., is the Chair of Alternative Programs and University Partnerships in the Graduate School of Education at Touro University, New York. She has over 14 years of experience in higher education, teaching courses in Science Education, Educational Technology, and Special Education. Prior to transitioning into higher education, Dr. Bobley was a middle and high school science teacher. Previously at Touro, Dr. Bobley served as Director of Graduate School of Education Online Education.

Sabra Brock, Ph.D., is Professor and Chair of the Business & Accounting Department at the New York School of Career and Applied Studies in Touro University, New York. She received a Ph.D. in Business Education from New York University, focusing on transformational learning. Dr. Brock publishes widely in scholarly journals. She co-founded the open innovation platform IdeaSpies.com in 2015. Her current research interest is the use of virtual reality in higher education. Prior to entering academia, Dr. Brock held global leadership positions at Citicorp, Colgate-Palmolive, DuPont, and Young & Rubicam.

Marcella Bullmaster-Day, Ed.D., M.A., M.Ed., is an Associate Professor at Touro University's Graduate School of Education. Her enduring interests are learning, teaching, and supporting others in learning and teaching. Her work has included roles as a youth clubs' director, teacher, school principal, research associate, curriculum designer, professional development consultant, and associate dean, all in urban educational contexts. She holds M.A., M.Ed., and Ed.D. degrees in Curriculum and Teaching from Teachers College, Columbia University.

Patricia Burke, Ph.D., C.N.E., R.N.C., is an Associate Professor at York College, City University of New York. Previously as the interim director of Nursing at Touro University, New York, she integrated interprofessional education throughout the undergraduate curriculum. Dr. Burke is originally from Ireland; she completed her nursing and midwifery studies in London, earned a baccalaureate degree from Pace University, New York, and a master's degree from Columbia University, New York. She completed her doctoral degree at Capella University. Dr. Burke's research interests include the use of technology, simulation, and interactive teaching strategies in nursing education.

Barbara A. Capozzi, D.O., C.N.S., serves as Clinical Dean of the Touro College of Osteopathic Medicine (Harlem, New York) and Associate Professor of Family Medicine. Her teaching experience spans the continuum of osteopathic medical education and interprofessional healthcare programs. She collaborated in the development of a Leadership Certificate program and has presented at state and national conferences. She completed the Touro College Academy of Leadership and Management Fellowship, collaborated on the establishment of the Touro Interdisciplinary Institute for Health Aging, and collaborated with colleagues at the Touro College of Pharmacy on leadership programs. Dr. Capozzi is the recipient of three leadership awards and the Teacher of the Year Award, reflecting her passion for excellence in medical education and promoting collaborative leadership.

Velma Cobb, Ed.D., C.P.C.C., A.C.C., is Director of the Lander Center for Educational Research and Associate Professor in the School Counseling Program in Touro University's Graduate School of Education. She is a certified leadership/emotional intelligence coach and skilled facilitator who looks at individual and organizational development through the lens of culture, neurobiology, and context. Dr. Cobb is a *Leadership Circle Profile (LCP)*© and *LCP Culture Survey*© 360 assessment practitioner, a *CARE* (Cultivating Awareness and Resilience in Educators) certified mindfulness facilitator, as well as a qualified administrator for the Intercultural Development Inventory (IDI) and the Conflict Styles Inventory (CSI).

Jasmin (Bey) Cowin, Ph.D., is an Associate Professor at Touro University, Fulbright Scholar, SIT Graduate, United States Department of State English Language Specialist (2024) in Assessment and Artificial Intelligence, and former Education Policy Fellow (EPFP™), Columbia University, Teachers College. Dr. Cowin regularly writes *Insights at the Intersection of AI and Education* for Stankevicius Media. Aligned with the United Nation's Sustainable Development Goal 4, she has contributed to initiatives such as Computers for Schools Burundi and TESOL "Train the Trainer" programs in Yemen and Morocco. Her research explores simulations for educators-in-training, AI in education and assessment, Metaverse applications, and educational transformation for language educators.

Charity Dacey, Ph.D., is the Associate Dean for Academic Affairs in the Graduate School of Education at Touro University. Dr. Dacey has 20 years of experience in higher education and has taught many courses in teacher education. She earned her Ph.D. in Teacher Education and Teacher Development from Montclair State University. Before transitioning to higher education, Dr. Dacey was a special education teacher. Like Nel Noddings (2010), Dr. Dacey believes that "Education, by its very nature, should help people to develop their best selves." Dr. Dacey leverages her skills to support public education by serving on the board of trustees for the Roseville Community Charter School.

Olga DeJesus-Diaz, Ed.D., is currently the Assistant Dean for Teacher Education and Associate Professor at Marist College. Her professional expertise extends beyond her teaching; she has made strides in service in the field of education. She has served as an expert for the United States Department of Education in initiatives to develop alternative assessments for English language learners, on the CEEDAR Taskforce with NYSED, and as a reviewer for the Association for Advancing Quality in Education Preparation (AAQEP). Dr. DeJesus-Diaz has shared her work both nationally and internationally. In 2017, as a Fulbright scholar, she presented at the University of Vienna, Austria, under the theme "Empowering the diverse learner through digital storytelling."

Carrie DiMatteo, Ph.D., is a Chair and Assistant Professor of Psychology at Touro University in New York. She earned her Ph.D. in Basic and Applied Social Psychology from the City University of New York Graduate Center. She teaches courses in Cognitive Psychology, Social Psychology, and Experimental Psychology. Dr. DiMatteo directs a research lab that combines the study of communication and the self. She has presented widely on the psychology of self-focused attention. Her research has combined eye tracking and online video chats to investigate self-focused attention. More recently, Dr. DiMatteo has studied the psychology of the self in social media.

Marius Fahrner, Ph.D., studied mathematics with a minor in philosophy and graduated from Humboldt University in Berlin with a thesis in quantum field theory. Dr. Fahrner wrote his dissertation on the application of the Socratic method in mathematics at the University of Cologne. Currently, he is a postdoc in Mathematics at Touro University Berlin, a campus of Touro University New York, with a special interest in learning theories and educational philosophy, and teaches courses in pure and applied mathematics as well as introductory courses in philosophy.

Shoshanah Findling, Ph.D., is the Site Director of the Graduate School of Education Brooklyn Campus of Touro University. She has been an assistant professor of Education for over 15 years, specializing in Early Childhood Education and School Counseling. Prior to this, she worked as a high school counselor specializing in post-secondary planning and related services for the New York City Department of Education. She earned her Master's of Education and Advanced Certificate in Guidance Counseling from Brooklyn College, Professional Certificate in School Administration from the College of St. Rose, and a Ph.D. in Career Counseling from Madison University.

Shmuel Fink, M.S., currently serves as an Associate Professor at Touro University. He earned his master's in computer science from Rochester Institute of Technology, followed by an Education Specialist and Doctorate in Computing Technology in Education from Nova Southeastern University. In addition to his extensive teaching experience, Dr. Fink chairs five master's programs within Touro's Graduate School of Technology and serves as deputy chair of the undergraduate Department of Computer Science. With over three decades in post-secondary education, he brings a wealth of expertise in leadership, administration, and teaching to these roles.

Gitta Jaroslawicz-Neufeld, M.A., coordinates Touro University's Jewish Childhood Education and Special Education Master's program, teaching methodology and technology while overseeing clinical practice. With a Master's Degree of Communications and a professional diploma in School Leadership, she is completing her doctorate in Educational Leadership. Previously, she directed teacher training at the Allegra Franco School of Educational Leadership and the Sephardic Rabbinical College and established the Herzog Collaborative for Judaic Studies teachers. Nationally recognized by the Covenant Foundation in 2012 as an outstanding educator, her interests lie in technology's impact on teaching and learning, and cultivating self-reflection and agency in educators.

Abraham M. Jeger, Ph.D., F.A.O.D.M., joined the faculty of New York Institute of Technology upon completing a Ph.D. in Psychology at SUNY Stony Brook and remained for an illustrious 41-year career. He assumed numerous academic and leadership positions, most notably serving as assistant/associate dean of Clinical Education at its medical school (NYITCOM), and professor of Psychiatry & Behavioral Medicine. His scholarly activities include a textbook on community mental health, journal articles, book chapters, and conference presentations. He received distinguished awards for: Rural Medical Education; Meritorious Clinical Education Service; Champion of Diversity; and a Special Lifetime Achievement Award. He currently serves as professor of Social, Behavioral, and Administrative Sciences at the Touro College of Pharmacy, where he collaborates on collaborative leadership curriculum development.

Anna Klippstein, Ph.D., is Professor of Finance and Dean of the M.B.A. Program at Touro University Berlin. Her field of competence covers Corporate Finance, International Financial Markets, Portfolio Analysis, International Management, Investment, Money & Banking, and Entrepreneurship. Before joining Touro Berlin in 2012, Dr. Klippstein worked at international banks such as UBS and LGT for more than 15 years. She is Ambassador for the Brain City, Berlin, executive member of the Diplomatic Club by the German Ministry of the Foreign Affairs, and member of the Academic Advisory Board of German Association of Small- and Medium-Sized Businesses.

Sarah J. Klugman, M.A., is the Director of Admissions and Recruitment for the Lander College for Women/The Anna Ruth and Mark Hasten School, which is an undergraduate division of Touro University. She has received her Master's in Marriage and Family Therapy from Touro University Worldwide. An accomplished high school teacher, college guidance counselor, and vice principal, she joined the Touro family 14 years ago as part of the administration of Lander College for Women and has helped the college grow yearly. Sarah is applying to programs to study for a Ph.D. in education administration.

Elina Lampert-Shepel, Ed.D., is an Associate Professor and Chair at Touro University. Previously, she taught NYC Teaching Fellows and collaborated with urban teachers, bringing innovative theory and practice to inner-city classrooms to create transformational learning experiences for diverse communities. Her research interests include cultural-historical psychology, activity theory, culture and cognition, communities of practice, and transformational change in education. Dr.

Lampert-Shepel conducted cross-cultural research on teacher reflexivity and transformative agency, working as a researcher and educator across Europe, the Middle East, and Brazil. Passionate about innovative programs and human development, she holds an Ed.D. degree from Teachers College, Columbia University.

Holger Luedeke, D.B.A., is professor of management at Touro University Berlin (a campus of Touro University New York). He teaches applied business classes in Berlin and New York and holds a doctorate in strategic management from the Free University of Berlin. In his doctoral thesis, he explored how a long-term perspective influences a company's strategic balance between defending its industry structure and opening to innovation. Prof. Luedeke's research areas are corporate governance; international corporate strategies; managerial human capital, organizational reputation; and the effects of spatial, socioeconomic, and temporal distance on professional networks. Dr. Luedeke is co-owner of the consulting agency INWISO, which specializes in measuring the impact of cross-border cooperation and estimating international and intra-national (regional) market demand, particularly in the healthcare sector.

Shamira Malekar, Ph.D., is a Professor of Business Management at the City University of New York—Borough of Manhattan Community College. Dr. Malekar has several research papers to her credit, published in national and international management journals of repute. She has received best paper awards at conferences in 2005, 2007, 2011, and 2012. She has authored a book entitled *Success with Emotional Intelligence*, published by Kendall Hunt Publishers, USA in 2017. The second edition of the book was released in 2020. Malekar was volume editor for three edited books comprising reviewed research papers presented at conferences in 2011, 2020, 2022.

Yair Maman, Ph.D., is the program chair of the Master of Science degree in School Counseling at the Graduate School of Education at Touro University. He holds a Ph.D. in Counseling Psychology from Hull University and a doctorate in psychotherapy from Middlesex University. He is a nationally certified counselor, a certified school psychologist, a certified school counselor, a licensed mental health counselor, and a licensed professional counselor. Dr. Maman has published extensively in the field of guidance and counseling. His research interests include, counselor education and supervision, perspectives of risky behavior in school-aged children, family and school collaboration, and the neglected and disadvantaged child.

Lenin Ortega, Ed.D., has worked at Touro University as an administrator for 20 plus years after serving in the United States Army. He earned his doctorate from the American College of Education, focusing on higher education. Currently, Dr. Ortega is an associate dean of academic affairs. He continues to focus on developing better administrative skills to become a well-rounded administrator.

Nilda Soto Ruiz, Ph.D., is currently Assistant Dean for Student Affairs and Professor and Chair of the School Leadership Program at the Touro University Graduate School of Education. She earned a baccalaureate degree from the City College of New York and master's and doctoral degrees from New York University. She has extensive experience as a teacher and high-ranking administrator in the New York City Public School System and has served as a Trustee of the City University of New York. Dr. Soto Ruiz's accomplishments have distinguished her as a leading practitioner and advocate in education. Her research interests include educational leadership and the teaching of English language learners.

Alan Sebel, Ed.D., is a Professor and Assistant Dean of Accreditation and Assessment at Touro University, New York. He has been a faculty member in the Graduate School of Education School Leadership program since 2003. He teaches courses in leadership and management to students seeking to be future school leaders. In his new position as assistant dean he will lead the Graduate School of Education's continuous improvement efforts. Dr. Sebel is a co-developer of the Touro College Academy of Leadership and Management. Prior to joining Touro, he was a deputy assistant superintendent in New York City public schools.

Marian Stotz-Loike, Ph.D., is a higher education thought leader who serves as the Dean of Touro's Lander College for Women/The Anna Ruth and Mark Hasten School (LCW) and as the Vice President for Online Education at Touro University. Dr. Stoltz-Loike has advised business leaders in the U.S. and North America, Europe, Asia, and South America. She has written two books and over fifty articles relating to remote education and diverse business issues. Dr. Stoltz-Loike is a popular speaker who has offered lectures on online education, higher education, business concerns, global leadership, and women's issues in the United States and around the world. She has been quoted in *BusinessWeek*, *BBC World*, and *Newsday*. She has been invited to blog for *US News and World Report* and other notable media.

Sara Tabaei, M.L.I.A., M.A., has been the Library Information Literacy Director at Touro University since 2007. She earned her master's degree in Library and Information Science from Wayne State University in Detroit, Michigan. In her diverse role, she manages outreach and represents the library in university-wide committees and events. Sara is responsible for overseeing the evaluation of the library's instructional program and works with faculty on various projects, including assessing students' information literacy skills. Sara initiated Touro Scholar, the institutional repository, and spearheaded the Open Educational Resources (OER) initiative along with the OER faculty fellowship. Beyond work, Sara enjoys hiking, traveling, and photography.

Ayushi Tandon, Ph.D., is Assistant Professor at the School of Management, Mahindra University, Hyderabad, India. Her Ph.D. research was ethnographic case studies to understand the utilization of electronic medical records in outpatient consultations for women's health. In addition, she has conducted experimental studies focusing on user engagement with mobile applications. Dr. Tandon is currently engaged in cross-country collaborations to explore the application of immersive technology in business education.

Thomas Troisi, Ed.D., is an Assistant Professor in the Department of School Leadership at Touro University. He has extensive P-12 school leadership experience and has served as an assistant principal, building principal, and assistant superintendent for Curriculum and Instruction on Long Island. Dr. Troisi earned his Ed.D. in Educational Administration and Policy Studies from Hofstra University. His articles concerning school leadership and technology have appeared in peer-reviewed journals, such as the *Teachers College Record* and the *School Administrator*. Dr. Troisi's academic interests include critical theory, instructional technology, and culturally responsive school leadership.

Elizabeth J. Unni, Ph.D., serves as Associate Professor and Chair of the Touro College of Pharmacy Department of Social, Behavioral, and Administrative Sciences. She holds leadership positions in various professional societies—most recently, Co-Editor-in-Chief of the *Journal of Patient-Reported Outcomes* (JPRO). Her extensive scholarly activities include preparing publications and presentations at national/international scientific meetings, particularly focusing on patients' self-management of chronic diseases. Dr. Unni is committed to fostering collaborative leadership in all her professional endeavors, including mentoring students and developing faculty. She is a "Leadership Institute Fellow" at the Society of Behavioral Medicine at Touro University and is a current Academy of Leadership Fellow with the American Association of Colleges of Pharmacy.

Luis Vidal, Ph.D., is the Chair of the department of anatomy at Touro University's College of Osteopathic Medicine in Harlem NY. Vidal is the course director of the Medical Histology course and participates as lecturing faculty in the embryology and neuroscience courses. He was the recipient of the Frank Grey Teacher of the Year award in 2020 for his commitment to medical education. Dr. Vidal earned his Ph.D. from the Department of Anatomy, Cell Biology, and Neuroscience at the University of Puerto Rico's Medical Sciences School. Dr. Vidal received post-doctoral training at Stony Brook University and at the City College of New York.

Laurie Wellner, Ed.D., is the Deputy Chair of the Education and Special Education program in the Graduate School of Education at Touro University in New York. She specializes in teacher education, autism, special education and organizational leadership, trust theory, and ethics in education. Dr. Wellner has over 30 years of experience, spanning from public school service in California as a general and special education teacher, autism specialist, and director of special education, as well as faculty and leadership positions in higher education.

Birgit Wolf, Ph.D., studied economics at University of Duisburg and completed higher education at the University of Hamburg. She worked as an underwriter and controller in reinsurance in the United Kingdom and Germany for 15 years before starting to teach at Touro University Berlin, a campus of Touro University New York in 2010. Since then, Dr. Wolf holds a professorship of management. Her special research interest is focused on comparative higher education.

Index